"Wrought was she of a painter's dream,—"

Memorial Edition

The Complete Works of

James Whitcomb Riley

IN TEN VOLUMES

Including Poems and Prose Sketches, many of which have not heretofore been published; an authentic Biography, an elaborate Index and numerous Illustrations from Paintings by Howard Chandler Christy and Ethel Franklin Betts

VOLUME I

WILDSIDE PRESS

TO

THE MEMORY OF

James Whitcomb Riley

AND

PLEASANT RECOLLECTION OF MORE THAN THIRTY-FIVE YEARS

OF BUSINESS AND PERSONAL ASSOCIATION

THESE FINAL VOLUMES

ARE AFFECTIONATELY DEDICATED

BORN:
October 7, 1849.
Greenfield, Ind.

DIED:
July 22, 1916
Indianapolis, Ind.

CONTENTS

PAGE

JAMES WHITCOMB RILEY—A SKETCH
A BACKWARD LOOK 23
PHILIPER FLASH 26
THE SAME OLD STORY............................ 30
TO A BOY WHISTLING............................ 32
AN OLD FRIEND.................................. 33
WHAT SMITH KNEW ABOUT FARMING............... 34
A POET'S WOOING 40
MAN'S DEVOTION................................. 42
A BALLAD 45
THE OLD TIMES WERE THE BEST.................. 49
A SUMMER AFTERNOON........................... 50
AT LAST.. 52
FARMER WHIPPLE—BACHELOR 54
MY JOLLY FRIEND'S SECRET...................... 62
THE SPEEDING OF THE KING'S SPITE.............. 65
JOB WORK 71
PRIVATE THEATRICALS 73
PLAIN SERMONS................................. 75
"TRADIN' JOE".................................. 76
DOT LEEDLE BOY................................ 81
I SMOKE MY PIPE............................... 86
RED RIDING HOOD............................... 88
IF I KNEW WHAT POETS KNOW.................... 89
AN OLD SWEETHEART OF MINE.................... 90
SQUIRE HAWKINS'S STORY........................ 95
A COUNTRY PATHWAY............................ 107
THE OLD GUITAR............................... 112
"FRIDAY AFTERNOON" 114
"JOHNSON'S BOY" 119
HER BEAUTIFUL HANDS.......................... 121
NATURAL PERVERSITIES......................... 123

CONTENTS

	PAGE
THE SILENT VICTORS	126
SCRAPS	132
AUGUST	134
DEAD IN SIGHT OF FAME	136
IN THE DARK	138
THE IRON HORSE	140
DEAD LEAVES	143
OVER THE EYES OF GLADNESS	145
ONLY A DREAM	147
OUR LITTLE GIRL	149
THE FUNNY LITTLE FELLOW	150
SONG OF THE NEW YEAR	153
A LETTER TO A FRIEND	155
LINES FOR AN ALBUM	156
TO ANNIE	157
FAME	158
AN EMPTY NEST	161
MY FATHER'S HALLS	162
THE HARP OF THE MINSTREL	163
HONEY DRIPPING FROM THE COMB	165
JOHN WALSH	166
ORLIE WILDE	168
THAT OTHER MAUD MULLER	176
A MAN OF MANY PARTS	178
THE FROG	180
DEAD SELVES	182
A DREAM OF LONG AGO	185
CRAQUEODOOM	188
JUNE	190
WASH LOWRY'S REMINISCENCE	191
THE ANCIENT PRINTERMAN	195
PRIOR TO MISS BELLE'S APPEARANCE	197
WHEN MOTHER COMBED MY HAIR	200
A WRANGDILLION	202
GEORGE MULLEN'S CONFESSION	204
"TIRED OUT"	213
HARLIE	214

CONTENTS

	PAGE
SAY SOMETHING TO ME	215
LEONAINIE	216
A TEST OF LOVE	218
FATHER WILLIAM	220
WHAT THE WIND SAID	222
MORTON	229
AN AUTUMNAL EXTRAVAGANZA	231
THE ROSE	233
THE MERMAN	235
THE RAINY MORNING	237
WE ARE NOT ALWAYS GLAD WHEN WE SMILE	238
A SUMMER SUNRISE	240
DAS KRIST KINDEL	242
AN OLD YEAR'S ADDRESS	247
A NEW YEAR'S PLAINT	249
LUTHER BENSON	252
"DREAM"	254
WHEN EVENING SHADOWS FALL	256
YLLADMAR	258
A FANTASY	260
A DREAM	264
DREAMER, SAY	266
BRYANT	268
BABYHOOD	269
LIBERTY	271
TOM VAN ARDEN	281

James Whitcomb Riley

JAMES WHITCOMB RILEY—A SKETCH

On Sunday morning, October seventh, 1849, Reuben A. Riley and his wife, Elizabeth Marine Riley, rejoiced over the birth of their second son. They called him James Whitcomb. This was in a shady little street in the shady little town of Greenfield, which is in the county of Hancock and the state of Indiana. The young James found a brother and a sister waiting to greet him—John Andrew and Martha Celestia, and afterward came Elva May—Mrs. Henry Eitel—Alexander Humbolt and Mary Elizabeth, who, of all, alone lives to see this collection of her brother's poems.

James Whitcomb was a slender lad, with corn-silk hair and wide blue eyes. He was shy and timid, not strong physically, dreading the cold of winter, and avoiding the rougher sports of his playmates. And yet he was full of the spirit of youth, a spirit that manifested itself in the performance of many ingenious pranks. His every-day life was that of the average boy in the average country town of that day, but his home influences were exceptional. His father, who became a captain of cavalry in the Civil War, was a lawyer of ability and an orator of more than local distinction. His mother was a woman of rare strength of character combined with deep sympathy and a clear understanding. Together, they made home a place to remember with thankin' heart. When James was twenty years old, the death of his mother made a profound impression on him, an impression that has influenced much of his verse and has remained with him always.

At an early age he was sent to school and, "then sent back again," to use his own words. He was restive under what he called the "iron discipline." A number of years ago, he spoke of these early educational beginnings in phrases so picturesque and so characteristic that they are quoted in full:

"My first teacher was a little old woman, rosy and roly-poly, who looked as though she might have just come tumbling out of a fairy story, so lovable was she and so jolly and so amiable. She kept school in her little Dame-Trot kind of dwelling of three rooms, with a porch in the rear, like a bracket on the wall, which was part of the playground of her 'scholars,'—for in those days pupils were called 'scholars' by their affectionate teachers. Among the twelve or fifteen boys and girls who were there I remember particularly a little lame boy, who always got the first ride in the locust-tree swing during recess.

"This first teacher of mine was a mother to all her 'scholars,' and in every way looked after their comfort, especially when certain little ones grew drowsy. I was often, with others, carried to the sitting-room and left to slumber on a small made-down pallet on the floor. She would sometimes take three or four of us together; and I recall how a playmate and I, having been admonished into silence, grew deeply interested in watching a spare old man who sat at a window with its shade drawn down. After a while we became accustomed to this odd sight and would laugh, and talk in whispers and give imitations, as we sat in a low sewing-chair, of the little old pendulating blind man at the window. Well, the old man was the gentle teacher's charge, and for this reason, possibly, her life had become an heroic one, caring for her helpless husband who, quietly content, waited always at the window for his sight to come back to him. And doubtless it is to-day, as he sits at another casement and sees not only his earthly friends, but all the friends of the Eternal Home, with the smiling, loyal, loving little woman forever at his side.

"She was the kindliest of souls even when constrained to punish us. After a whipping she invariably took me into the little kitchen and gave me two great white slabs of bread cemented together with layers of butter and jam. As she always whipped me with the same slender switch she used for a pointer, and cried over every lick, you will have an idea how much punishment I could stand. When I was old enough to be lifted by the ears out of my seat that office was performed by a pedagogue whom I promised to 'whip sure, if he'd just wait till I got big enough.' He is still waiting!

"There was but one book at school in which I found the slightest interest: McGuffey's old leather-bound Sixth Reader. It was the tallest book known, and to the boys of my size it was a matter of eternal wonder how I could belong to 'the big class in that reader.' When we were to read the death of 'Little Nell,' I would run away, for I knew it would make me cry, that the other boys would laugh at me, and the whole thing would become ridiculous. I couldn't bear that. A later teacher, Captain Lee O. Harris, came to understand me with thorough sympathy, took compassion on my weaknesses and encouraged me to read the best literature. He understood that he couldn't get numbers into my head. You couldn't tamp them in! History I also disliked as a dry thing without juice, and dates melted out of my memory as speedily as tin-foil on a red-hot stove. But I always was ready to declaim and took natively to anything dramatic or theatrical. Captain Harris encouraged me in recitation and reading and had ever the sweet spirit of a companion rather than the manner of an instructor."

But if there was "only one book at school in which he found the slightest interest," he had before that time displayed an affection for a book—simply as such and not for any printed word it might contain. And this, after all, is the true book-lover's love. Speaking of this incident—and he liked to refer to it as his "first literary recollection," he said: "Long before I was old enough to read I remember buying a book at an old auctioneer's shop in Greenfield. I can not imagine what prophetic impulse took possession of me and made me forego the ginger cakes and the candy that usually took every cent of my youthful income. The slender little volume must have cost all of twenty-five cents! It was Francis Quarles' *Divine Emblems,*—a neat little affair about the size of a pocket Testament. I carried it around with me all day long, delighted with the very feel of it.

" 'What have you got there, Bub?' some one would ask. 'A book,' I would reply. 'What kind of a book?' 'Poetry-book.' 'Poetry!' would be the amused exclamation. 'Can you read poetry?' and, embarrassed, I'd shake my head and make my escape, but I held on to the beloved little volume."

Every boy has an early determination—a first one —to follow some ennobling profession, once he has come to man's estate, such as being a policeman, or a performer on the high trapeze. The poet would not have been the "People's Laureate," had his fairy god-mother granted his boy-wish, but the Greenfield baker. For to his childish mind it "seemed the acme of delight," using again his own happy expression, "to manufacture those snowy loaves of bread, those delicious tarts, those toothsome bon-bons. And then to own them all, to keep them in store, to watch over and guardedly exhibit. The thought of getting

money for them was to me a sacrilege. Sell them?
No indeed. Eat 'em—eat 'em, by tray loads and
dray loads! It was a great wonder to me why the
pale-faced baker in our town did not eat all his good
things. This I determined to do when I became
owner of such a grand establishment. Yes, sir. I
would have a glorious feast. Maybe I'd have Tom
and Harry and perhaps little Kate and Florry in to
help us once in a while. The thought of these playmates as 'grown-up folks' didn't appeal to me. I
was but a child, with wide-open eyes, a healthy appetite and a wondering mind. That was all. But I
have the same sweet tooth to-day, and every time I
pass a confectioner's shop, I think of the big baker
of our town, and Tom and Harry and the youngsters all."

As a child, he often went with his father to the
court-house where the lawyers and clerks playfully
called him "Judge Wick." Here as a privileged
character he met and mingled with the country folk
who came to sue and be sued, and thus early the
dialect, the native speech, the quaint expressions of
his "own people" were made familiar to him, and
took firm root in the fresh soil of his young memory.
At about this time, he made his first poetic attempt
in a valentine which he gave to his mother. Not
only did he write the verse, but he drew a sketch
to accompany it, greatly to his mother's delight, who
according to the best authority, gave the young poet
"three big cookies and didn't spank me for two

weeks. This was my earliest literary encouragement."

Shortly after his sixteenth birthday, young Riley turned his back on the little schoolhouse and for a time wandered through the different fields of art, indulging a slender talent for painting until he thought he was destined for the brush and palette, and then making merry with various musical instruments, the banjo, the guitar, the violin, until finally he appeared as bass drummer in a brass band. "In a few weeks," he said, "I had beat myself into the more enviable position of snare drummer. Then I wanted to travel with a circus, and dangle my legs before admiring thousands over the back seat of a Golden Chariot. In a dearth of comic songs for the banjo and guitar, I had written two or three myself, and the idea took possession of me that I might be a clown, introduced as a character-song-man and the composer of my own ballads.

"My father was thinking of something else, however, and one day I found myself with a 'five-ought' paint brush under the eaves of an old frame house that drank paint by the bucketful, learning to be a painter. Finally, I graduated as a house, sign and ornamental painter, and for two summers traveled about with a small company of young fellows calling ourselves 'The Graphics,' who covered all the barns and fences in the state with advertisements."

At another time his young man's fancy saw attractive possibilities in the village print-shop, and later his ambition was diverted to acting, encouraged by the good times he had in the theatricals of the Adelphian Society of Greenfield. "In my dreamy way," he afterward said, "I did a little of a number of things fairly well—sang, played the guitar and violin, acted, painted signs and wrote poetry. My father did not encourage my verse-making for he thought it too visionary, and being a visionary himself, he believed he understood the dangers of following the promptings of the poetic temperament. I doubted if anything would come of the verse-writing myself. At this time it is easy to picture my father, a lawyer of ability, regarding me, nonplused, as the worst case he had ever had. He wanted me to do something practical, besides being ambitious for me to follow in his footsteps, and at last persuaded me to settle down and read law in his office. This I really tried to do conscientiously, but finding that political economy and Blackstone did not rhyme and that the study of law was unbearable, I slipped out of the office one summer afternoon, when all outdoors called imperiously, shook the last dusty premise from my head and was away.

"The immediate instigator of my flight was a traveling medicine man who appealed to me for this reason: My health was bad, very bad,—as bad as I was. Our doctor had advised me to travel, but how could I travel without money? The medicine man needed an assistant and I plucked up courage to ask

A—1

if I could join the party and paint advertisements for him.

"I rode out of town with that glittering cavalcade without saying good-by to any one, and though my patron was not a diplomaed doctor, as I found out, he was a man of excellent habits, and the whole company was made up of good straight boys, jolly chirping vagabonds like myself. It was delightful to bowl over the country in that way. I laughed all the time. Miles and miles of somber landscape were made bright with merry song, and when the sun shone and all the golden summer lay spread out before us, it was glorious just to drift on through it like a wisp of thistle-down, careless of how, or when, or where the wind should anchor us. 'There's a tang of gipsy blood in my veins that pants for the sun and the air.'

"My duty proper was the manipulation of two blackboards, swung at the sides of the wagon during our street lecture and concert. These boards were alternately embellished with colored drawings illustrative of the manifold virtues of the nostrum vended. Sometimes I assisted the musical olio with dialect recitations and character sketches from the back step of the wagon. These selections in the main originated from incidents and experiences along the route, and were composed on dull Sundays in lonesome little towns where even the church bells seemed to bark at us."

A—2

On his return to Greenfield after this delightful but profitless tour he became the local editor of his home paper and in a few months "strangled the little thing into a change of ownership." The new proprietor transferred him to the literary department and the latter, not knowing what else to put in the space allotted him, filled it with verse. But there was not room in his department for all he produced, so he began, timidly, to offer his poetic wares in foreign markets. The editor of *The Indianapolis Mirror* accepted two or three shorter verses but in doing so suggested that in the future he try prose. Being but an humble beginner, Riley harkened to the advice, whereupon the editor made a further suggestion; this time that he try poetry again. *The Danbury* (Connecticut) *News,* then at the height of its humorous reputation, accepted a contribution shortly after *The Mirror* episode and Mr. McGeechy, its managing editor, wrote the young poet a graceful note of congratulation. Commenting on these parlous times, Riley afterward wrote, "It is strange how little a thing sometimes makes or unmakes a fellow. In these dark days I should have been content with the twinkle of the tiniest star, but even this light was withheld from me. Just then came the letter from McGeechy; and about the same time, arrived my first check, a payment from *Hearth and Home* for a contribution called *A Destiny* (now *A Dreamer* in *A Child World*). The letter was signed, 'Editor' and unless

sent by an assistant it must have come from Ik
Marvel himself, God bless him! I thought my
fortune made. Almost immediately I sent off another contribution, whereupon to my dismay came
this reply: 'The management has decided to discon-
tinue the publication and hopes that you will find
a market for your worthy work elsewhere.' Then
followed dark days indeed, until finally, inspired by
my old teacher and comrade, Captain Lee O. Harris,
I sent some of my poems to Longfellow, who replied in his kind and gentle manner with the sub-
stantial encouragement for which I had long
thirsted."

In the year following, Riley formed a connection
with *The Anderson* (Indiana) *Democrat* and con-
tributed verse and locals in more than generous
quantities. He was happy in this work and had begun to feel that at last he was making progress
when evil fortune knocked at his door and, conspiring with circumstances and a friend or two, in-
duced the young poet to devise what afterward
seemed to him the gravest of mistakes,—the Poe-
poem hoax. He was then writing for an audience
of county papers and never dreamed that this
whimsical bit of fooling would be carried beyond
such boundaries. It was suggested by these circumstances. He was inwardly distressed by the belief
that his failure to get the magazines to accept his
verse was due to his obscurity, while outwardly he
was harassed to desperation by the junior editor of

the rival paper who jeered daily at his poetical pretensions. So, to prove that editors would praise from a known source what they did not hesitate to condemn from one unknown, and to silence his nagging contemporary, he wrote *Leonainie* in the style of Poe, concocting a story, to accompany the poem, setting forth how Poe came to write it and how all these years it had been lost to view. In a few words Mr. Riley related the incident and then dismissed it. "I studied Poe's methods. He seemed to have a theory, rather misty to be sure, about the use of 'm's' and 'n's' and mellifluous vowels and sonorous words. I remember that I was a long time in evolving the name *Leonainie,* but at length the verses were finished and ready for trial.

"A friend, the editor of *The Kokomo Dispatch,* undertook the launching of the hoax in his paper; he did this with great editorial gusto while, at the same time, I attacked the authenticity of the poem in *The Democrat.* That diverted all possible suspicion from me. The hoax succeeded far too well, for what had started as a boyish prank became a literary discussion nation-wide, and the necessary exposé had to be made. I was appalled at the result. The press assailed me furiously, and even my own paper dismissed me because I had given the 'discovery' to a rival."

Two dreary and disheartening years followed this tragic event, years in which the young poet found no present help, nor future hope. But over in Indianapolis, twenty miles away, happier circumstances were shaping themselves. Judge E. B. Martindale, editor and proprietor of *The Indianapolis Journal,* had been attracted by certain poems in various papers over the state and at the very time that the poet was ready to confess himself beaten, the judge wrote: "Come over to. Indianapolis and we'll give you a place on *The Journal.*" Mr. Riley went. That was the turning point, and though the skies were not always clear, nor the way easy, still from that time it was ever an ascending journey. As soon as he was comfortably settled in his new position, the first of the Benj. F. Johnson poems made its appearance. These dialect verses were introduced with editorial comment as coming from an old Boone county farmer, and their reception was so cordial, so enthusiastic, indeed, that the business manager of *The Journal,* Mr. George C. Hitt, privately published them in pamphlet form and sold the first edition of one thousand copies in local bookstores and over *The Journal* office counter. This marked an epoch in the young poet's progress and was the beginning of a friendship between him and Mr. Hitt that has never known interruption. This first edition of *The Old Swimmin' Hole and 'Leven More Poems* has since become extremely rare and now commands a high premium. A second edition was promptly issued by a local book dealer, whose successors, The Bowen-Merrill Company—now The Bobbs-Merrill Company—have continued, practically without interruption, to publish Riley's work.

The call to read from the public platform had by this time become so insistent that Riley could no longer resist it, although modesty and shyness fought the battle for privacy. He told briefly and in his own inimitable fashion of these trying experiences. "In boyhood I had been vividly impressed with Dickens' success in reading from his own works and dreamed that some day I might follow his example. At first I read at Sunday-school entertainments and later, on special occasions such as Memorial Days and Fourth of Julys. At last I mustered up sufficient courage to read in a city theater, where, despite the conspiracy of a rainy night and a circus, I got encouragement enough to lead me to extend my efforts. And so, my native state and then the country at large were called upon to bear with me and I think I visited every sequestered spot north or south particularly distinguished for poor railroad connections. At different times, I shared the program with Mark Twain, Robert J. Burdette and George Cable, and for a while my gentlest and cheeriest of friends, Bill Nye, joined with me and made the dusty detested travel almost a delight. We were constantly playing practical jokes on each other or indulging in some mischievous banter before the audience. On one occasion, Mr. Nye, coming before the footlights for a word of general introduction, said,

'Ladies and gentlemen, the entertainment to-night is of a dual nature. Mr. Riley and I will speak alternately. First I come out and talk until I get tired, then Mr. Riley comes out and talks until *you* get tired!' And thus the trips went merrily enough at times and besides I learned to know in Bill Nye a man blessed with as noble and heroic a heart as ever beat. But the making of trains, which were all in conspiracy to outwit me, schedule or no schedule, and the rush and tyrannical pressure of inviolable engagements, some hundred to a season and from Boston to San Francisco, were a distress to my soul. I am glad that's over with. Imagine yourself on a crowded day-long excursion; imagine that you had to ride all the way on the platform of the car; then imagine that you had to ride all the way back on the same platform; and lastly, try to imagine how you would feel if you did that every day of your life, and you will then get a glimmer—a faint glimmer—of how one feels after traveling about on a reading or lecturing tour.

"All this time I had been writing whenever there was any strength left in me. I could not resist the inclination to write. It was what I most enjoyed doing. And so I wrote, laboriously ever, more often using the rubber end of the pencil than the point.

"In my readings I had an opportunity to study and find out for myself what the public wants, and afterward I would endeavor to use the knowledge gained in my writing. The public desires nothing but what is absolutely natural, and so perfectly natural as to be fairly artless. It can not tolerate affectation, and it takes little interest in the classical production. It demands simple sentiments that come direct from the heart. While on the lecture platform I watched the effect that my readings had on the audience very closely and whenever anybody left the hall I knew that my recitation was at fault, and tried to find out why. Once a man and his wife made an exit while I was giving *The Happy Little Cripple*—a recitation I had prepared with particular enthusiasm and satisfaction. It fulfilled, as few poems do, all the requirements of length, climax and those many necessary features for a recitation. The subject was a theme of real pathos, beautified by the cheer and optimism of the little sufferer. Consequently when this couple left the hall I was very anxious to know the reason and asked a friend to find out. He learned that they had a little hunchback child of their own. After this experience I never used that recitation again. On the other hand, it often required a long time for me to realize that the public would enjoy a poem which, because of some blind impulse, I thought unsuitable. Once a man said to me, 'Why don't you recite *When the Frost Is on the Punkin?*' The use of it had never occurred to me for I thought it 'wouldn't go.' He persuaded me to try it and it became one of my most favored recitations. Thus, I learned to judge and value my verses by their effect upon the public. Occasionally, at first, I had presumed to write 'over the heads' of the audience, consoling myself for the cool reception by thinking my auditors were not of sufficient intellectual height to appreciate my efforts. But after a time it came home to me that I myself was at fault in these failures, and then I disliked anything that did not appeal to the public and learned to discriminate between that which did not ring true to my hearers and that which won them by virtue of its truthfulness and was simply heart high."

As a reader of his own poems, as a teller of humorous stories, as a mimic, indeed as a finished actor, Riley's genius was rare and beyond question. In a lecture on the Humorous Story, Mark Twain, referring to the story of the *One Legged Soldier* and the different ways of telling it, once said:

"It takes only a minute and a half to tell it in its comic form; and it isn't worth telling after all. Put into the humorous-story form, it takes ten minutes, and is about the funniest thing I have ever listened to—as James Whitcomb Riley tells it.

"The simplicity and innocence and sincerity and unconsciousness of Riley's old farmer are perfectly simulated, and the result is a performance which is thoroughly charming and delicious. This is art —and fine and beautiful, and only a master can compass it."

It was in 1883 that *The Old Swimmin' Hole*

and 'Leven More Poems first appeared in volume form. Four years afterward, Riley made his initial appearance before a New York City audience. The entertainment was given in aid of an international copyright law, and the country's most distinguished men of letters took part in the program. It is probably true that no one appearing at that time was less known to the vast audience in Chickering Hall than James Whitcomb Riley, but so great and so spontaneous was the enthusiasm when he left the stage after his contribution to the first day's program, that the management immediately announced a place would be made for Mr. Riley on the second and last day's program. It was then that James Russell Lowell introduced him in the following words:

"Ladies and gentlemen: I have very great pleasure in presenting to you the next reader of this afternoon, Mr. James Whitcomb Riley, of Indiana. I confess, with no little chagrin and sense of my own loss, that when yesterday afternoon, from this platform, I presented him to a similar assemblage, I was almost completely a stranger to his poems. But since that time I have been looking into the volumes that have come from his pen, and in them I have discovered so much of high worth and tender quality that I deeply regret I had not long before made acquaintance with his work. To-day, in presenting Mr. Riley to you, I can say to you of my own knowledge, that you are to have the pleasure of listening to the voice of a true poet."

Two years later a selection from his poems was published in England under the title *Old Fashioned Roses* and his international reputation was established. In his own country the people had already conferred their highest degrees on him and now the colleges and universities—seats of conservatism—gave him scholastic recognition. Yale made him an Honorary Master of Arts in 1902; in 1903, Wabash and, a year later, the University of Pennsylvania conferred on him the degree of Doctor of Letters, and in 1907 Indiana University gave him his LL. D. Still more recently the Academy of Arts and Letters elected him to membership, and in 1912 awarded him the gold medal for poetry. About this time a yet dearer, more touching tribute came to him from school children. On October 7, 1911, the schools of Indiana and New York City celebrated his birthday by special exercises, and one year later, the school children of practically every section of the country had programs in his honor.

As these distinguished honors came they found him each time surprised anew and, though proud that they who dwell in the high places of learning should come in cap and gown to welcome him, yet gently and sincerely protesting his own unworthiness. And as they found him when they came so they left him.

Mr. Riley made his home in Indianapolis from the time Judge Martindale invited him to join *The Journal's* forces, and no one of her citizens was more devoted, nor was any so universally loved and honored. Everywhere he went the tribute of quick recognition and cheery greeting was paid him, and his home was the shrine of every visiting Hoosier. High on a sward of velvet grass stands a dignified middle-aged brick house. A dwarfed stone wall, broken by an iron gate, guards the front lawn, while in the rear an old-fashioned garden revels in hollyhocks and wild roses. Here among his books and his souvenirs the poet spent his happy and contented days. To reach this restful spot, the pilgrim must journey to Lockerbie Street, a miniature thoroughfare half hidden between two more commanding avenues. It is little more than a lane, shaded, unpaved and from end to end no longer than a five minutes' walk, but its fame is for all time.

"Such a dear little street it is, nestled away
From the noise of the city and heat of the day,
In cool shady coverts of whispering trees,
With their leaves lifted up to shake hands with the
    breeze
Which in all its wide wanderings never may meet
With a resting-place fairer than Lockerbie Street!"

Riley never married. He lived with devoted, loyal and understanding friends, a part of whose life he became many years ago. Kindly consideration, gentle affection, peace and order,—all that go to make home home, were found here blooming with the hollyhocks and the wild roses. Every day some visitor knocked for admittance and was not denied; every day saw the poet calling for some companionable friend and driving with him through the city's shaded streets or far out into the country.

And so his life drew on to its last and most beautiful year. Since his serious illness in 1910, the public had shown its love for him more and more frequently. On the occasion of his birthday in 1912, Greenfield had welcomed him home through a host of children scattering flowers. Anderson, where he was living when he first gained public recognition, had a Riley Day in 1913. The Indiana State University entertained him the same year, as did also the city of Cincinnati. In 1915 there was a Riley Day at Columbus, Indiana, and during all this time each birthday and Christmas was marked by "poetry-showers," and by thousands of letters of affectionate congratulation and by many tributes in the newspapers and magazines.

His last birthday, October 7, 1915, was the most notable of all. Honorable Franklin K. Lane, Secretary of the Interior, suggested to the various school superintendents that one of Riley's poems be read in each schoolhouse, with the result that Riley celebrations were general among the children of the entire country. In a proclamation by Governor Ralston the State of Indiana designated the anniversary as Riley Day in honor of its "most beloved citizen." Thousands of letters and gifts from the poet's friends poured in—letters from schools and

organizations and Riley Clubs as well as from in-
dividuals—while flowers came from every section
of the country. Among them all, perhaps the poet
was most pleased with a bunch of violets picked
from the banks of the Brandywine by the children
of a Riley school.

It was on this last birthday that an afternoon
festival of Riley poems set to music and danced
in pantomime took place at Indianapolis. This was
followed at night by a dinner in his honor at which
Charles Warren Fairbanks presided, and the speak-
ers were Governor Ralston, Doctor John Finley,
Colonel George Harvey, Young E. Allison, William
Allen White, George Ade, Ex-Senator Beveridge
and Senator Kern. That night Riley smiled his
most wonderful smile, his dimpled boyish smile, and
when he rose to speak it was with a perceptible
quaver in his voice that he said: "Everywhere the
faces of friends, a beautiful throng of friends!"

The winter and spring following, Riley spent
quietly at Miami, Florida, where he had gone the
two previous seasons to escape the cold and the rain.
There was a Riley Day at Miami in February. In
April, he returned home, feeling at his best, and,
as if by premonition, sought out many of his
friends, new and old, and took them for last rides
in his automobile. A few days before the end, he
visited Greenfield to attend the funeral of a dear
boyhood chum, Almon Keefer, of whom he wrote
in *A Child-World*. All Riley's old friends who

were still left in Greenfield were gathered there
and to them he spoke words of faith and good cheer.
Almon Keefer had "just slipped out" quietly and
peacefully, he said, and "it was beautiful."

And as quietly and peacefully his own end came
—as he had desired it, with no dimming of the fac-
ulties even to the very close, nor suffering, nor con-
fronting death. This was Saturday night, July 22,
1916. On Monday afternoon and evening his body
lay in state under the dome of Indiana's capitol,
while the people filed by, thousands upon thousands.
Business men were there, and schoolgirls, matrons
carrying market baskets, mothers with little children, here and there a swarthy foreigner, old folks,
too, and well-dressed youths, here a farmer and his
wife, and there a workman in a blue jumper with
his hat in his hand, silent, inarticulate, yet bidding
his good-by, too. On the following day, with only
his nearest and dearest about him, all that was mortal of the people's poet was quietly and simply laid
to rest.

The Complete Works of James Whitcomb Riley

A BACKWARD LOOK

A S I sat smoking, alone, yesterday,
And lazily leaning back in my chair,
Enjoying myself in a general way—
Allowing my thoughts a holiday
  From weariness, toil and care,—
My fancies—doubtless, for ventilation—
  Left ajar the gates of my mind,—
And Memory, seeing the situation,
  Slipped out in the street of "Auld Lang Syne."—

Wandering ever with tireless feet
  Through scenes of silence, and jubilee
Of long-hushed voices; and faces sweet
Were thronging the shadowy side of the street
  As far as the eye could see;
Dreaming again, in anticipation,
  The same old dreams of our boyhood's days
That never come true, from the vague sensation
  Of walking asleep in the world's strange ways.

23

Away to the house where I was born!
    And there was the selfsame clock that ticked
From the close of dusk to the burst of morn,
When life-warm hands plucked the golden corn
    And helped when the apples were picked.
And the "chany dog" on the mantel-shelf,
    With the gilded collar and yellow eyes,
Looked just as at first, when I hugged myself
    Sound asleep with the dear surprise.

And down to the swing in the locust-tree,
    Where the grass was worn from the trampled
        ground,
And where "Eck" Skinner, "Old" Carr, and three
Or four such other boys used to be
    "Doin' sky-scrapers," or "whirlin' round":
And again Bob climbed for the bluebird's nest,
    And again "had shows" in the buggy-shed
Of Guymon's barn, where still, unguessed,
    The old ghosts romp through the best days dead!

And again I gazed from the old schoolroom
    With a wistful look, of a long June day,
When on my cheek was the hectic bloom
Caught of Mischief, as I presume—
    He had such a "partial" way,
It seemed, toward me.—And again I thought
    Of a probable likelihood to be
Kept in after school—for a girl was caught
    Catching a note from me.

"Again I gazed from the old schoolroom"

And down through the woods to the swimming-
          hole—
  Where the big, white, hollow old sycamore
          grows,—
And we never cared when the water was cold,
And always "ducked" the boy that told
  On the fellow that tied the clothes.—
When life went so like a dreamy rhyme,
  That it seems to me now that then
The world was having a jollier time
  Than it ever will have again.

PHILIPER FLASH

YOUNG Philiper Flash was a promising lad,
 His intentions were good—but oh, how sad
  For a person to think
  How the veriest pink
And bloom of perfection may turn out bad.
Old Flash himself was a moral man,
And prided himself on a moral plan,
  Of a maxim as old
  As the calf of gold,
Of making that boy do what he was told.

And such a good mother had Philiper Flash;
Her voice was as soft as the creamy plash
  Of the milky wave
  With its musical lave
That gushed through the holes of her patent churn-
        dash;—
And the excellent woman loved Philiper so,
She could cry sometimes when he stumped his toe,—
  And she stroked his hair
  With such motherly care
When the dear little angel learned to swear.

Old Flash himself would sometimes say
That his wife had "such a ridiculous way,—
　　She'd humor that child
　　Till he'd soon be sp'iled,
And then there'd be the devil to pay!"
And the excellent wife, with a martyr's look,
Would tell old Flash himself "he took
　　No notice at all
　　Of the bright-eyed doll
Unless when he spanked him for getting a fall!"

Young Philiper Flash, as time passed by,
Grew into "a boy with a roguish eye":
　　He could smoke a cigar,
　　And seemed by far
The most promising youth.—"He's powerful sly,"
Old Flash himself once told a friend,
"Every copper he gets he's sure to spend—
　　And," said he, "don't you know
　　If he keeps on so
What a crop of wild oats the boy will grow!"

But his dear good mother knew Philiper's ways
So—well, she managed the money to raise;
　　And old Flash himself
　　Was "laid on the shelf,"
(In the manner of speaking we have nowadays).
For "gracious knows, her darling child,
If he went without money he'd soon grow wild."
　　So Philiper Flash

With a regular dash
"Swung on to the reins," and went "slingin' the
      cash."

As old Flash himself, in his office one day,
Was shaving notes in a barberous way,
   At the hour of four
   Death entered the door
And shaved the note on his life, they say.
And he had for his grave a magnificent tomb,
Though the venturous finger that pointed "Gone
         Home,"
   Looked white and cold
   From being so bold,
As it feared that a popular lie was told.

Young Philiper Flash was a man of style
When he first began unpacking the pile
   Of the dollars and dimes
   Whose jingling chimes
Had clinked to the tune of his father's smile;
And he strewed his wealth with such lavish hand,
His rakish ways were the talk of the land,
   And gossipers wise
   Sat winking their eyes
(A certain foreboding of fresh surprise).

A "fast young man" was Philiper Flash,
And wore "loud clothes" and a weak mustache,
   And "done the Park,"

For an "afternoon lark,"
With a very fast horse of "remarkable dash."
And Philiper handled a billiard-cue
About as well as the best he knew,
   And used to say
   "He could make it pay
By playing two or three games a day."

And Philiper Flash was his mother's joy,
He seemed to her the magic alloy
   That made her glad,
   When her heart was sad,
With the thought that "she lived for her darling
      boy."
His dear good mother wasn't aware
How her darling boy relished a "tare."—
   She said "one night
   He gave her a fright
By coming home late and *acting* tight."

Young Philiper Flash, on a winterish day,
Was published a bankrupt, so they say—
   And as far as I know
   I suppose it was so,
For matters went on in a singular way;
His excellent mother, I think I was told,
Died from exposure and want and cold;
   And Philiper Flash,
   With a horrible slash,
Whacked his jugular open and went to smash.

THE SAME OLD STORY

THE same old story told again—
  The maiden droops her head,
The ripening glow of her crimson cheek
  Is answering in her stead.
The pleading tone of a trembling voice
  Is telling her the way
He loved her when his heart was young
  In Youth's sunshiny day:
The trembling tongue, the longing tone,
  Imploringly ask why
They can not be as happy now
  As in the days gone by.
And two more hearts, tumultuous
  With overflowing joy,
Are dancing to the music
  Which that dear, provoking boy
Is twanging on his bowstring,
  As, fluttering his wings,
He sends his love-charged arrows
  While merrily he sings:

"Ho! ho! my dainty maiden,
  It surely can not be
You are thinking you are master
  Of your heart, when it is me."
And another gleaming arrow
  Does the little god's behest,
And the dainty little maiden
  Falls upon her lover's breast.
"The same old story told again,"
  And listened to o'er and o'er,
Will still be new, and pleasing, too,
  Till "Time shall be no more."

TO A BOY WHISTLING

THE smiling face of a happy boy
   With its enchanted key
  Is now unlocking in memory
My store of heartiest joy.

And my lost life again to-day,
   In pleasant colors all aglow,
   From rainbow tints, to pure white snow,
Is a panorama sliding away.

The whistled air of a simple tune
   Eddies and whirls my thoughts around,
   As fairy balloons of thistle-down
Sail through the air of June.

O happy boy with untaught grace!
   What is there in the world to give
   That can buy one hour of the life you live
Or the trivial cause of your smiling face!

AN OLD FRIEND

HEY, Old Midsummer! are you here again,
　　With all your harvest-store of olden joys,—
Vast overhanging meadow-lands of rain,
And drowsy dawns, and noons when golden grain
　　Nods in the sun, and lazy truant boys
Drift ever listlessly adown the day,
Too full of joy to rest, and dreams to play.

The same old Summer, with the same old smile
　　Beaming upon us in the same old way
We knew in childhood! Though a weary while
Since that far time, yet memories reconcile
　　The heart with odorous breaths of clover hay;
And again I hear the doves, and the sun streams
　　　　through
The old barn door just as it used to do.

And so it seems like welcoming a friend—
　　An old, *old* friend, upon his coming home
From some far country—coming home to spend
Long, loitering days with me: And I extend
　　My hand in rapturous glee:—And so you've
　　　　come!—
Ho, I'm so glad! Come in and take a chair:
Well, this is just like *old* times, I declare!

WHAT SMITH KNEW ABOUT FARMING

THERE wasn't two purtier farms in the state
   Than the couple of which I'm about to relate;—
Jinin' each other—belongin' to Brown,
And jest at the edge of a flourishin' town.
Brown was a man, as I understand,
That allus had handled a good 'eal o' land,
And was sharp as a tack in drivin' a trade—
For that's the way most of his money was made.
And all the grounds and the orchards about
His two pet farms was all tricked out
With poppies and posies
And sweet-smellin' rosies;
And hundreds o' kinds
Of all sorts o' vines,
To tickle the most horticultural minds;
And little dwarf trees not as thick as your wrist
With ripe apples on 'em as big as your fist:
And peaches—Siberian crabs and pears
And quinces—Well! *any* fruit *any* tree bears;
And the purtiest stream—jest a-swimmin' with fish
And—*jest a'most everything heart could wish!*
The purtiest orch'rds—I wish you could see
How purty they was, fer I know it 'ud be
A regular treat!—but I'll go ahead with
My story! A man by the name o' Smith—

(A bad name to rhyme,
But I reckon that I'm
Not goin' back on a Smith! nary time!)
'At hadn't a soul of kin nor kith,
And more money than he knowed what to do with,—
So he comes a-ridin' along one day,
And *he* says to Brown, in his offhand way—
Who was trainin' some newfangled vines round a
          bay-
Winder—"Howdy-do—look-a-here—say:
What'll you take fer this property here?—
I'm talkin' o' leavin' the city this year,
And I want to be
Where the air is free,
And I'll *buy* this place, if it ain't too dear!"—
Well—they grumbled and jawed aroun'—
"I don't like to part with the place," says Brown;
"Well," says Smith, a-jerkin' his head,
"That house yonder—bricks painted red—
Jest like this'n—a *purtier view*—
Who is it owns *it?*" "That's mine too,"
Says Brown, as he winked at a hole in his shoe,
"But I'll tell you right here jest what I *kin* do:—
If you'll pay the figgers I'll sell *it* to you."
Smith went over and looked at the place—
Badgered with Brown, and argied the case—
Thought that Brown's figgers was rather too tall,
But, findin' that Brown wasn't goin' to fall,
In final agreed,
So they drawed up the deed

Fer the farm and the fixtures—the live stock an' all.
And so Smith moved from the city as soon
As he possibly could—But "the man in the moon"
Knowed more'n Smith o' farmin' pursuits,
And jest to convince you, and have no disputes,
How little he knowed,
I'll tell you his "mode,"
As he called it, o' raisin' "the best that growed,"
In the way o' potatoes—
Cucumbers—tomatoes,
And squashes as lengthy as young alligators.
'Twas allus a curious thing to me
How big a fool a feller kin be
When he gits on a farm after leavin' a town!—
Expectin' to raise himself up to renown,
And reap fer himself agricultural fame,
By growin' of squashes—*without any shame*—
As useless and long as a technical name.
To make the soil pure,
And certainly sure,
He plastered the ground with patent manure.
He had cultivators, and double-hoss plows,
And patent machines fer milkin' his cows;
And patent hay-forks—patent measures and
        weights,
And new patent back-action hinges fer gates,
And barn locks and latches, and such little dribs,
And patents to keep the rats out o' the cribs—
Reapers and mowers,
And patent grain sowers;

And drillers
And tillers
And cucumber hillers,
And horries;—and had patent rollers and scrapers,
And took about ten agricultural papers.
So you can imagine how matters turned out:
But *Brown* didn't have not a shadder o' doubt
That Smith didn't know what he was about
When he said that "the *old* way to farm was played
      out."
But Smith worked ahead,
And when any one said
That the *old* way o' workin' was better instead
O' his "modern idees," he allus turned red,
And wanted to know
What made people so
Infernally anxious to hear theirselves crow?
And guessed that he'd manage to hoe his own row.
Brown he come onc't and leant over the fence,
And told Smith that he couldn't see any sense
In goin' to such a tremendous expense
Fer the sake o' such no-account experiments:—
"That'll never make corn!
As shore's you're born
It'll come out the leetlest end of the horn!"
Says Brown, as he pulled off a big roastin'-ear
From a stalk of his own
That had tribble outgrown
Smith's poor yaller shoots, and says he, "Looky
      here!

This corn was raised in the old-fashioned way,
And I rather imagine that *this* corn'll pay
Expenses fer *raisin'* it!—What do you say?"
Brown got him then to look over his crop.—
His luck that season had been tip-top!
And you may surmise
Smith opened his eyes
And let out a look o' the wildest surprise
When Brown showed him punkins as big as the lies
He was stuffin' him with—about offers he's had
Fer his farm: "I don't want to sell very bad,"
He says, but says he,
"Mr. Smith, you kin see
Fer yourself how matters is standin' with me,
I understand farmin' and I'd better stay,
You know, on my farm;—I'm a-makin' it pay—
I oughtn't to grumble!—I reckon I'll clear
Away over four thousand dollars this year."
And that was the reason, he made it appear,
Why he didn't care about sellin' his farm,
And hinted at his havin' done himself harm
In sellin' the other, and wanted to know
If Smith wouldn't sell back ag'in to him.—So
Smith took the bait, and says he, "Mr. Brown,
I wouldn't *sell* out but we might swap aroun'—
How'll you trade your place fer mine?"
(Purty sharp way o' comin' the shine
Over Smith! Wasn't it?) Well, sir, this Brown
Played out his hand and brought Smithy down—
Traded with him an', workin' it cute,

Raked in two thousand dollars to boot
As slick as a whistle, an' that wasn't all,—
He managed to trade back ag'in the next fall,—
And the next—and the next—as long as Smith
        stayed
He reaped with his harvests an annual trade—
Why, I reckon that Brown must 'a' easily made—
On an *average*—nearly two thousand a year—
Together he made over seven thousand—clear.—
Till Mr. Smith found he was losin' his health
In as big a proportion, almost, as his wealth;
So at last he concluded to move back to town,
And sold back his farm to this same Mr. Brown
At very low figgers, by gittin' it down.
Further'n this I have nothin' to say
Than merely advisin' the Smiths fer to stay
In their grocery stores in flourishin' towns
And leave agriculture alone—and the Browns.

A—4

A POET'S WOOING

I woo'd a woman once,
But she was sharper than an eastern wind.

—TENNYSON.

"WHAT may I do to make you glad,
　　To make you glad and free,
　Till your light smiles glance
　And your bright eyes dance
Like sunbeams on the sea?
　　Read some rhyme that is blithe and gay
　　Of a bright May morn and a marriage day?"
And she sighed in a listless way she had,—
"Do not read—it will make me sad!"

"What shall I do to make you glad—
　To make you glad and gay,
　　Till your eyes gleam bright
　　As the stars at night
When as light as the light of day?—
　　Sing some song as I twang the strings
　　Of my sweet guitar through its wanderings?"
And she sighed in the weary way she had,—
"Do not sing—it will make me sad!"

40

"What can I do to make you glad—
　As glad as glad can be,
　　Till your clear eyes seem
　　Like the rays that gleam
　And glint through a dew-decked tree?—
　　Will it please you, dear, that I now begin
　　A grand old air on my violin?"
And she spoke again in the following way,—
　　"Yes, oh yes, it would please me, sir;
　I would be so glad you'd play
　　Some grand old march—in character,—
　And then as you march away
I will no longer thus be sad,
But oh, so glad—so glad—so glad!"

MAN'S DEVOTION

A LOVER said, "O Maiden, love me well,
  For I must go away:
And should *another* ever come to tell
  Of love—What *will* you say?"

And she let fall a royal robe of hair
  That folded on his arm
And made a golden pillow for her there;
  Her face—as bright a charm

As ever setting held in kingly crown—
  Made answer with a look,
And reading it, the lover bended down,
  And, trusting, "kissed the book."

He took a fond farewell and went away.
  And slow the time went by—
So weary—dreary was it, day by day
  To love, and wait, and sigh.

She kissed his pictured face sometimes, and
    said:
"O Lips, so cold and dumb,
I would that you would tell me, if not dead,
    Why, why do you not come?"

The picture, smiling, stared her in the face
    Unmoved—e'en with the touch
Of tear-drops—*hers*—bejeweling the case—
    'Twas plain—she loved him much.

And, thus she grew to think of him as gay
    And joyous all the while,
And *she* was sorrowing—"Ah, welladay!"
    But pictures *always* smile!

And years—dull years—in dull monotony
    As ever went and came,
Still weaving changes on unceasingly,
    And changing, changed her name.

Was she untrue?—She oftentimes was glad
    And happy as a wife;
But *one* remembrance oftentimes made sad
    Her matrimonial life.—

Though its few years were hardly noted, when
    Again her path was strown
With thorns—the roses swept away again,
    And she again alone!

And then—alas! ah *then!*—her lover came:
  "I come to claim you now—
My Darling, for I know *you* are the same,
  And I have kept *my* vow

Through these long, long, long years, and now
      no more
  Shall we asundered be!"
She staggered back and, sinking to the floor,
  Cried in her agony:

"I have been false!" she moaned, "*I* am not
      true—
  I am not worthy now,
Nor even can I be a wife to *you*—
  For I have broke my vow!"

And as she kneeled there, sobbing at his feet,
  He calmly spoke—no sign
Betrayed his inward agony—"I count you meet
  To be a wife of mine!"

And raised her up forgiven, though untrue;
  As fond he gazed on her,
She sighed,—"*So happy!*" And she never
      knew
  He was a *widower*.

A BALLAD

WITH A SERIOUS CONCLUSION

CROWD about me, little children—
  Come and cluster 'round my knee
While I tell a little story
  That happened once with me.

My father he had gone away
  A-sailing on the foam,
Leaving me—the merest infant—
  And my mother dear at home;

For my father was a sailor,
  And he sailed the ocean o'er
For full five years ere yet again
  He reached his native shore.

And I had grown up rugged
  And healthy day by day,
Though I was but a puny babe
  When father went away.

Poor mother she would kiss me
  And look at me and sigh
So strangely, oft I wondered
  And would ask the reason why.

45

And she would answer sadly,
  Between her sobs and tears,—
"You look so like your father,
  Far away so many years!"

And then she would caress me
  And brush my hair away,
And tell me not to question,
  But to run about my play.

Thus I went playing thoughtfully—
  For that my mother said,—
"You look so like your father!"
  Kept ringing in my head.

So, ranging once the golden sands
  That looked out on the sea,
I called aloud, "My father dear,
  Come back to ma and me!"

Then I saw a glancing shadow
  On the sand, and heard the shriek
Of a sea-gull flying seaward,
  And I heard a gruff voice speak:—

"Ay, ay, my little shipmate,
  I thought I heard you hail;
Were you trumpeting that sea-gull,
  Or do you see a sail?"

And as rough and gruff a sailor
　As ever sailed the sea
Was standing near grotesquely
　And leering dreadfully.

I replied, though I was frightened,
　"It was my father dear
I was calling for across the sea—
　I think he didn't hear."

And then the sailor leered again
　In such a frightful way,
And made so many faces
　I was little loathe to stay:

But he started fiercely toward me—
　Then made a sudden halt
And roared, *"I think he heard you!"*
　And turned a somersault.

Then a wild fear overcame me,
　And I flew off like the wind,
Shrieking *"Mother!"*—and the sailor
　Just a little way behind!

And then my mother heard me,
　And I saw her shade her eyes,
Looking toward me from the doorway,
　Transfixed with pale surprise

For a moment—then her features
  Glowed with all their wonted charms
As the sailor overtook me,
  And I fainted in her arms.

When I awoke to reason
  I shuddered with affright
Till I felt my mother's presence
  With a thrill of wild delight—

Till, amid a shower of kisses
  Falling glad as summer rain,
A muffled thunder rumbled,—
  "Is he coming 'round again?"

Then I shrieked and clung unto her,
  While her features flushed and burned
As she told me it was father
  From a foreign land returned.

      .   .   .   .

I said—when I was calm again,
  And thoughtfully once more
Had dwelt upon my mother's words
  Of just the day before,—

"I *don't* look like my father,
  As you told me yesterday—
I know I don't—or father
  Would have run the other way."

THE OLD TIMES WERE THE BEST

FRIENDS, my heart is half aweary
　Of its happiness to-night:
Though your songs are gay and cheery,
　And your spirits feather-light,
There's a ghostly music haunting
　Still the heart of every guest
And a voiceless chorus chanting
　That the Old Times were the best.

CHORUS

All about is bright and pleasant
　With the sound of song and jest,
Yet a feeling's ever present
　That the Old Times were the best.

A SUMMER AFTERNOON

A LANGUID atmosphere, a lazy breeze,
   With labored respiration, moves the wheat
From distant reaches, till the golden seas
   Break in crisp whispers at my feet.

My book, neglected of an idle mind,
   Hides for a moment from the eyes of men;
Or, lightly opened by a critic wind,
   Affrightedly reviews itself again.

Off through the haze that dances in the shine
   The warm sun showers in the open glade,
The forest lies, a silhouette design
   Dimmed through and through with shade.

A dreamy day; and tranquilly I lie
   At anchor from all storms of mental strain;
With absent vision, gazing at the sky,
   "Like one that hears it rain."

The Katydid, so boisterous last night,
  Clinging, inverted, in uneasy poise,
Beneath a wheat-blade, has forgotten quite
  If "Katy *did* or *didn't*" make a noise.

The twitter, sometimes, of a wayward bird
  That checks the song abruptly at the sound,
And mildly, chiding echoes that have stirred,
  Sink into silence, all the more profound.

And drowsily I hear the plaintive strain
  Of some poor dove . . . Why, I can
      scarcely keep
My heavy eyelids—there it is again—
  "Coo-coo!"—I mustn't—"Coo-coo!"—fall
      asleep!

AT LAST

A DARK, tempestuous night; the stars shut in
    With shrouds of fog; an inky, jet-black blot
The firmament; and where the moon has been
    An hour agone seems like the darkest spot.
The weird wind—furious at its demon game—
Rattles one's fancy like a window-frame.

A care-worn face peers out into the dark,
    And childish faces—frightened at the gloom—
Grow awed and vacant as they turn to mark
    The father's as he passes through the room:
The gate latch clatters, and wee baby Bess
Whispers, "The doctor's tummin' now, I dess!"

The father turns; a sharp, swift flash of pain
    Flits o'er his face: "Amanda, child! I said
A moment since—I see I must *again*—
    Go take your little sisters off to bed!
There, Effie, Rose, and *Clara mustn't cry!*"
"I tan't he'p it—I'm fyaid 'at mama'll die!"

What are his feelings, when this man alone
   Sits in the silence, glaring in the grate
That sobs and sighs on in an undertone
   As stoical—immovable as Fate,
While muffled voices from the sick one's room
Come in like heralds of a dreaded doom?

The door-latch jingles: in the doorway stands
   The doctor, while the draft puffs in a breath—
The dead coals leap to life, and clap their hands,
   The flames flash up. A face as pale as death
Turns slowly—teeth tight clenched, and with a look
The doctor, through his specs, reads like a book.

"Come, brace up, Major!"—"Let me know the
    worst!"
   "W'y you're the biggest fool I ever saw—
Here, Major—take a little brandy first—
   There! She's a *boy*—I mean *he* is—hurrah!"
"Wake up the other girls—and shout for joy—
Eureka is his name—I've found A BOY!"

FARMER WHIPPLE—BACHELOR

IT'S a mystery to see me—a man o' fifty-four,
  Who's lived a cross old bachelor fer thirty year',
      and more—
A-lookin' glad and smilin'! And they's none o' you
      can say
That you can guess the reason why I feel so good
      to-day!

I must tell you all about it! But I'll have to deviate
A little in beginnin', so's to set the matter straight
As to how it comes to happen that I never took a
      wife—
Kindo' "crawfish" from the Present to the Spring-
      time of my life!

I was brought up in the country: Of a family of
      five—
Three brothers and a sister—I'm the only one
      alive,—
Fer they all died little babies; and 'twas one o'
      Mother's ways,
You know, to want a daughter; so she took a girl
      to raise.

54

The sweetest little thing she was, with rosy cheeks,
    and fat—
We was little chunks o' shavers then about as high
    as that!
But someway we sort o' *suited*-like! and Mother
    she'd declare
She never laid her eyes on a more lovin' pair

Than *we* was! So we growed up side by side fer
    thirteen year',
And every hour of it she growed to me more
    dear!—
W'y, even Father's dyin', as he did, I do believe
Warn't more affectin' to me than it was to see her
    grieve!

I was then a lad o' twenty; and I felt a flash o'
    pride
In thinkin' all depended on *me* now to pervide
Fer Mother and fer Mary; and I went about the
    place
With sleeves rolled up—and workin', with a mighty
    smilin' face.—

Fer *somepin' else* was workin'! but not a word I said
Of a certain sort o' notion that was runnin' through
    my head,—
"Some day I'd maybe marry, and a *brother's* love
    was one
Thing—a *lover's* was another!" was the way the
    notion run!

A—5

I remember onc't in harvest, when the "cradle-in' "
  was done,
(When the harvest of my summers mounted up to
  twenty-one),
I was ridin' home with Mary at the closin' o' the
  day—
A-chawin' straws and thinkin', in a lover's lazy
  way!

And Mary's cheeks was burnin' like the sunset
  down the lane:
I noticed she was thinkin', too, and ast her to
  explain.
Well—when she turned and *kissed* me, *with her
  arms around me—law!*
I'd a bigger load o' Heaven than I had a load o'
  straw!

I don't p'tend to learnin', but I'll tell you what's a
  fac',
They's a mighty truthful sayin' somers in a'
  almanac—
Er *somers*—'bout "puore happiness"—perhaps
  some folks'll laugh
At the idy—"only lastin' jest two seconds and a
  half."—

But it's jest as true as preachin'!—fer that was a
  sister's kiss,
And a sister's lovin' confidence a-tellin' to me
  this:—

"*She* was happy, *bein' promised to the son o'*
    Farmer Brown."—
And my feelin's struck a pardnership with sunset
    and went down!

I don't know *how* I acted, and I don't know *what*
    I said,—
Fer my heart seemed jest a-turnin' to an ice-cold
    lump o' lead;
And the hosses kind o' glimmered before me in the
    road,
And the lines fell from my fingers—And that was
    all I knowed—

Fer—well, I don't know *how* long—They's a dim
    rememberence
Of a sound o' snortin' horses, and a stake-and-
    ridered fence
A-whizzin' past, and wheat-sheaves a-dancin' in the
    air,
And Mary screamin' "Murder!" and a-runnin' up
    to where

I was layin' by the roadside, and the wagon upside
    down
A-leanin' on the gate-post, with the wheels
    a-whirlin' roun'!
And I tried to raise and meet her, but I couldn't,
    with a vague
Sort o' notion comin' to me that I had a broken leg.

Well, the women nussed me through it; but many a
    time I'd sigh
As I'd keep a-gittin' better instid o' goin' to die,
And wonder what was left *me* worth livin' fer
    below,
When the girl I loved was married to another,
    don't you know!

And my thoughts was as rebellious as the folks
    was good and kind
When Brown and Mary married—Railly must 'a'
    been my *mind*
Was kind o' out o' kilter!—fer I hated Brown, you
    see,
Worse'n *pizen*—and the feller whittled crutches
    out fer *me*—

And done a thousand little ac's o' kindness and
    respec'—
And me a-wishin' all the time that I could break his
    neck!
My relief was like a mourner's when the funeral is
    done
When they moved to Illinois in the Fall o' Forty-
    one.

Then I went to work in airnest—I had nothin' much
    in view
But to drownd out rickollections—and it kep' me
    busy, too!

But I slowly thrived and prospered, tel Mother used
    to say
She expected yit to see me a wealthy man some day.

Then I'd think how little *money* was, compared to
    happiness—
And who'd be left to use it when I died I couldn't
    guess!
But I've still kep' speculatin' and a-gainin' year by
    year,
Tel I'm payin' half the taxes in the county, mighty
    near!

Well!—A year ago er better, a letter comes to hand
Astin' how I'd like to dicker fer some Illinois land—
"The feller that had owned it," it went ahead to
    state,
"Had jest deceased, insolvent, leavin' chance to
    speculate,"—

And then it closed by sayin' that I'd "better come
    and see."—
I'd never been West, anyhow—a'most too wild fer
    me,
I'd allus had a notion; but a lawyer here in town
Said I'd find myself mistakend when I come to
    look around.

So I bids good-by to Mother, and I jumps aboard
    the train,
A-thinkin' what I'd bring her when I come back
    home again—

And ef she'd had an idy what the present was to be,
I think it's more'n likely she'd 'a' went along with
    me!

Cars is awful tejus ridin', fer all they go so fast!
But finally they called out my stoppin'-place at last:
And that night, at the tavern, I dreamp' I was a
    train
O' cars, and *skeered* at somepin', runnin' down a
    country lane!

Well, in the morning airly—after huntin' up the
    man—
The lawyer who was wantin' to swap the piece o'
    land—
We started fer the country; and I ast the history
Of the farm—its former owner—and so forth,
    etcetery!

And—well—it was inter*es*tin'—I su'prised him, I
    suppose,
By the loud and frequent manner in which I blowed
    my nose!—
But his su'prise was greater, and it made him won-
    der more,
When I kissed and hugged the widder when she
    met us at the door!—

"They'd never seed their grandma—and I fetched
'em home with me"

It was Mary: . . . They's a feelin' a-hidin' down
    in here—
Of course I can't explain it, ner ever make it
    clear.—
It was with us in that meetin', I don't want you to
    fergit!
And it makes me kind o' nervous when I think about
    it yit!

I *bought* that farm, and *deeded* it, afore I left the
    town,
With "title clear to mansions in the skies," to Mary
    Brown!
And fu'thermore, I took her and the *childern*—fer
    you see,
They'd never seed their Grandma—and I fetched
    'em home with me.

So *now* you've got an idy why a man o' fifty-four,
Who's lived a cross old bachelor fer thirty year' and
    more,
Is a-lookin' glad and smilin'!—And I've jest come
    into town
To git a pair o' license fer to *marry* Mary Brown.

MY JOLLY FRIEND'S SECRET

A H, friend of mine, how goes it
    Since you've taken you a mate?—
Your smile, though, plainly shows it
    Is a very happy state!
Dan Cupid's necromancy!
    You must sit you down and dine,
And lubricate your fancy
    With a glass or two of wine.

And as you have "deserted,"
    As my other chums have done,
While I laugh alone diverted,
    As you drop off one by one—
And I've remained unwedded,
    Till—you see—look here—that I'm,
In a manner, "snatched bald-headed"
    By the sportive hand of Time!

I'm an "old 'un!" yes, but wrinkles
    Are not so plenty, quite,
As to cover up the twinkles
    Of the *boy*—ain't I right?

Yet, there are ghosts of kisses
   Under this mustache of mine
My mem'ry only misses
   When I drown 'em out with wine.

From acknowledgment so ample,
   You would hardly take me for
What I am—a perfect sample
   Of a "jolly bachelor";
Not a bachelor has being
   When he laughs at married life
But his heart and soul's agreeing
   That he ought to have a wife!

Ah, ha! old chum, this claret,
   Like Fatima, holds the key
Of the old Blue-Beardish garret
   Of my hidden mystery!
Did you say you'd like to listen?
   Ah, my boy! the *"Sad No More!"*
And the tear-drops that will glisten—
   Turn the catch upon the door,

And sit you down beside me,
   And put yourself at ease—
I'll trouble you to slide me
   That wine decanter, please;
The path is kind o' mazy
   Where my fancies have to go,
And my heart gets sort o' lazy
   On the journey—don't you know?

Let me see—when I was twenty—
  It's a lordly age, my boy,
When a fellow's money's plenty,
  And the leisure to enjoy—
And a girl—with hair as golden
  As—*that;* and lips—well—quite
As red as *this* I'm holdin'
  Between you and the light.

And eyes and a complexion—
  Ah, heavens!—le'-me-see—
Well,—just in this connection,—
  Did you lock that door for me?
Did I start in recitation
  My past life to recall?
Well, *that's* an indication
  I am purty tight—that's all!

THE SPEEDING OF THE KING'S SPITE

A KING—estranged from his loving Queen
   By a foolish royal whim—
Tired and sick of the dull routine
   Of matters surrounding him—
Issued a mandate in this wise:—
   "The dower of my daughter's hand
I will give to him who holds this prize,
   The strangest thing in the land."

But the King, sad sooth! in this grim decree
   Had a motive low and mean;—
'Twas a royal piece of chicanery
   To harry and spite the Queen;
For King though he was, and beyond compare,
   He had ruled all things save one—
Then blamed the Queen that his only heir
   Was a daughter—not a son.

The girl had grown, in the mother's care,
   Like a bud in the shine and shower
That drinks of the wine of the balmy air
   Till it blooms into matchless flower;

Her waist was the rose's stem that bore
  The flower—and the flower's perfume—
That ripens on till it bulges o'er
  With its wealth of bud and bloom.

And she had a lover—lowly sprung,—
  But a purer, nobler heart
Never spake in a courtlier tongue
  Or wooed with a dearer art:
And the fair pair paled at the King's decree;
  But the smiling Fates contrived
To have them wed, in a secrecy
  That the Queen *herself* connived—

While the grim King's heralds scoured the land
  And the countries roundabout,
Shouting aloud, at the King's command,
  A challenge to knave or lout,
Prince or peasant,—"The mighty King
  Would have ye understand
That he who shows him the strangest thing
  Shall have his daughter's hand!"

And thousands flocked to the royal throne,
  Bringing a thousand things
Strange and curious;—One, a bone—
  The hinge of a fairy's wings;
And one, the glass of a mermaid queen,
  Gemmed with a diamond dew,
Where, down in its reflex, dimly seen,
  Her face smiled out at you.

One brought a cluster of some strange date,
  With a subtle and searching tang
That seemed, as you tasted, to penetrate
  The heart like a serpent's fang;
And back you fell for a spell entranced,
  As cold as a corpse of stone,
And heard your brains, as they laughed and
    danced
  And talked in an undertone.

One brought a bird that could whistle a tune
  So piercingly pure and sweet,
That tears would fall from the eyes of the moon
  In dewdrops at its feet;
And the winds would sigh at the sweet refrain,
  Till they swooned in an ecstacy,
To waken again in a hurricane
  Of riot and jubilee.

One brought a lute that was wrought of a shell
  Luminous as the shine
Of a new-born star in a dewy dell,—
  And its strings were strands of wine
That sprayed at the Fancy's touch and fused,
  As your listening spirit leant
Drunken through with the airs that oozed
  From the o'ersweet instrument.

One brought a tablet of ivory
  Whereon no thing was writ,—
But, at night—and the dazzled eyes would see
  Flickering lines o'er it,—

And each, as you read from the magic tome,
  Lightened and died in flame,
And the memory held but a golden poem
  Too beautiful to name.

Till it seemed all marvels that ever were known
  Or dreamed of under the sun
Were brought and displayed at the royal throne,
  And put by, one by one;—
Till a graybeard monster came to the King—
  Haggard and wrinkled and old—
And spread to his gaze this wondrous thing,—
  A gossamer veil of gold.—

Strangely marvelous—mocking the gaze
  Like a tangle of bright sunshine,
Dipping a million glittering rays
  In a baptism divine:
And a maiden, sheened in this gauze attire—
  Sifting a glance of her eye—
Dazzled men's souls with a fierce desire
  To kiss and caress her and—die.

And the grim King swore by his royal beard
  That the veil had won the prize,
While the gray old monster blinked and leered
  With his lashless, red-rimmed eyes,
As the fainting form of the princess fell,
  And the mother's heart went wild,
Throbbing and swelling a muffled knell
  For the dead hopes of her child.

But her clouded face with a faint smile shone,
  As suddenly, through the throng,
Pushing his way to the royal throne,
  A fair youth strode along,
While a strange smile hovered about his eyes,
  As he said to the grim old King:—
"The veil of gold must lose the prize;
  For *I* have a stranger thing."

He bent and whispered a sentence brief;
  But the monarch shook his head,
With a look expressive of unbelief—
  "It can't be so," he said;
"Or give me proof; and I, the King,
  Give you my daughter's hand,—
For certes THAT *is* a stranger thing—
  The strangest thing in the land!"

Then the fair youth, turning, caught the Queen
  In a rapturous caress,
While his lithe form towered in lordly mien,
  As he said in a brief address:—
"My fair bride's mother is this; and, lo,
  As you stare in your royal awe,
By this pure kiss do I proudly show
  A love for a mother-in-law!"

Then a thaw set in the old King's mood,
  And a sweet Spring freshet came
Into his eyes, and his heart renewed
  Its love for the favored dame:

But often he has been heard to declare
That "he never could clearly see
How, in the deuce, such a strange affair
Could have ended so happily!"

JOB WORK

"WRITE me a rhyme of the present time";
　　And the poet took his pen
And wrote such lines as the miser minds
　　Hide in the hearts of men.

He grew enthused, as the poets used
　　When their fingers kissed the strings
Of some sweet lyre, and caught the fire
　　True inspiration brings,

And sang the song of a nation's wrong—
　　Of the patriot's galling chain,
And the glad release that the angel, Peace,
　　Has given him again.

He sang the lay of religion's sway,
　　Where a hundred creeds clasp hands
And shout in glee such a symphony
　　That the whole world understands.

71

He struck the key of monopoly,
  And sang of her swift decay,
And traveled the track of the railway back
  With a blithesome roundelay—

Of the tranquil bliss of a true love kiss;
  And painted the picture, too,
Of the wedded life, and the patient wife,
  And the husband fond and true;

And sang the joy that a noble boy
  Brings to a father's soul,
Who lets the wine as a mocker shine
  Stagnated in the bowl.

And he stabbed his pen in the ink again,
  And wrote, with a writhing frown,
"This is the end." "And now, my friend,
  You may print it—upside down!"

PRIVATE THEATRICALS

A QUITE convincing axiom
    Is, "Life is like a play";
For turning back its pages some
    Few dog-eared years away,
        I find where I
        Committed my
Love-tale—with brackets where to sigh.

I feel an idle interest
    To read again the page;
I enter, as a lover dressed,
    At twenty years of age,
        And play the part
        With throbbing heart,
And all an actor's glowing art.

And she who plays my Lady-love
    Excels!—Her loving glance
Has power her audience to move—
    I am her audience.—
        Her acting tact,
        To tell the fact,
"Brings down the house" in every act.

And often we defy the curse
  Of storms and thunder-showers,
To meet together and rehearse
  This little play of ours—
    I think, when she
    "Makes love" to me,
She kisses very naturally!

    ·   ·   ·   ·   ·   ·

Yes; it's convincing—rather—
  That "Life is like a play":
I am playing "Heavy Father"
  In a "Screaming Farce" to-day,
    That so "brings down
    The house," I frown,
And fain would "ring the curtain down."

PLAIN SERMONS

I SAW a man—and envied him beside—
   Because of this world's goods he had great
     store;
But even as I envied him, he died,
   And left me envious of him no more.

I saw another man—and envied still—
   Because he was content with frugal lot;
But as I envied him, the rich man's will
   Bequeathed him all, and envy I forgot.

Yet still another man I saw, and he
   I envied for a calm and tranquil mind
That nothing fretted in the least degree—
   Until, alas! I found that he was blind.

What vanity is envy! for I find
   I have been rich in dross of thought, and poor
In that I was a fool, and lastly blind—
   For never having seen myself before!

75

"TRADIN' JOE"

I'M one o' these cur'ous kind o' chaps
   You think you know when you don't,
      perhaps!
I hain't no fool—ner I don't p'tend
To be so smart I could rickommend
Myself fer a *congerssman,* my friend!—
But I'm kind o' betwixt-and-between, you
        know,—
One o' these fellers 'at folks call "slow."
And I'll say jest here I'm kind o' queer
Regardin' things 'at I *see* and *hear,*—
Fer I'm *thick* o' hearin' *sometimes,* and
It's hard to git me to understand;
But other times it hain't, you bet!
Fer I don't sleep with both eyes shet!

I've swapped a power in stock, and so
The neighbers calls me "Tradin' Joe"—
And I'm goin' to tell you 'bout a trade,—
And one o' the best I ever made:

Folks has gone so fur's to say
'At I'm well fixed, in a *worldly* way,
And *bein'* so, and a *widower,*
It's not su'prisin', as you'll infer,
I'm purty handy among the sect—

76

Widders especially, rickollect!
And I won't deny that along o' late
I've hankered a heap fer the married state—
But some way o' 'nother the longer we wait
The harder it is to discover a mate.

Marshall Thomas,—a friend o' mine,
Doin' some in the tradin' line,
But a'most too *young* to know it all—
On'y at *picnics* er some *ball!*—
Says to me, in a banterin' way,
As we was a-loadin' stock one day,—
"You're a-huntin' a wife, and I want you to see
My girl's mother, at Kankakee!—
She hain't over forty—good-lookin' and spry,
And jest the woman to fill your eye!
And I'm a-goin' there Sund'y,—and now,"
      says he,
"I want to take you along with *me;*
And you marry *her,* and," he says, "by 'shaw!
You'll hev me fer yer son-in-law!"
I studied a while, and says I, "Well, I'll
First have to see ef she suits my style;
And ef she does, you kin bet your life
Your mother-in-law will be my wife!"

Well, Sund'y come; and I fixed up some—
Putt on a collar—I did, by gum!—
Got down my "plug," and my satin vest—
(You wouldn't know me to see me dressed!—

But any one knows ef you got the clothes
You kin go in the crowd wher' the best of 'em
          goes!)
And I greeced my boots, and combed my hair
Keerfully over the bald place there;
And Marshall Thomas and me that day
Eat our dinners with Widder Gray
And her girl Han'!   *   *   *

                Well, jest a glance
O' the widder's smilin' countenance,
A-cuttin' up chicken and big pot-pies,
Would make a man hungry in Paradise!
And passin' p'serves and jelly and cake
'At would make an *angel's* appetite *ache!*—
Pourin' out coffee as yaller as gold—
Twic't as much as the cup could hold—
La! it was rich!—And then she'd say,
"Take some o' *this!*" in her coaxin' way,
Tell ef I'd been a hoss I'd 'a' *foundered*, shore,
And jest dropped dead on her white-oak floor!

Well, the way I talked would 'a' done you good,
Ef you'd 'a' been there to 'a' understood;
Tel I noticed Hanner and Marshall, they
Was a-noticin' me in a cur'ous way;
So I says to myse'f, says I, "Now, Joe,
The best thing fer you is to jest go slow!"
And I simmered down, and let them do
The bulk o' the talkin' the evening through.

And Marshall was still in a talkative gait
When he left, that evening—tolable late.
"How do you like her?" he says to me;
Says I, "She suits, to a 't-y-*Tee*'!"
And then I ast how matters stood
With him in the *opposite* neighberhood?
"Bully!" he says; "I ruther guess
I'll finally git her to say the 'yes.'
I named it to her to-night, and she
Kind o' smiled, and said *'she'd see'*—
And that's a purty good sign!" says he:
"Yes," says I, "you're ahead o' *me!*"
And then he laughed, and said, *"Go in!"*
And patted me on the shoulder ag'in.

Well, ever sense then I've been ridin' a good
Deal through the Kankakee neighberhood;
And I make it convenient sometimes to stop
And hitch a few minutes, and kind o' drop
In at the widder's, and talk o' the crop
And one thing o' 'nother. And week afore last
The notion struck me, as I drove past,
I'd stop at the place and state my case—
Might as well do it at first as last!

I felt first-rate; so I hitched at the gate,
And went up to the house; and, strange to
     relate,
Marshall Thomas had dropped in, *too.*—
"Glad to see you, sir, how do you do?"
He says, says he! Well—it *sounded queer:*

And when Han' told me to take a cheer,
Marshall got up and putt out o' the room—
And motioned his hand fer the *widder* to come.
I didn't say nothin' fer quite a spell,
But thinks I to myse'f, "There's a dog in the
        well!"
And Han' *she* smiled so cur'ous at me—
Says I, "What's up?"   And she says, says she,
"Marshall's been at me to marry ag'in,
And I told him 'no,' jest as you come in."
Well, somepin' o' 'nother in that girl's voice
Says to me, "Joseph, here's your choice!"
And another minute her guileless breast
Was lovin'ly throbbin' ag'in my vest!—
And then I kissed her, and heerd a smack
Come like a' echo a-flutterin' back,
And we looked around, and in full view
Marshall was kissin' the widder, too!
Well, we all of us laughed, in our glad su'prise,
Tel the tears come *a-streamin'* out of our eyes!
And when Marsh said " 'Twas the squarest
        trade
That ever me and him had made,"
We both shuck hands, 'y jucks! and swore
We'd stick together ferevermore.
And old Squire Chipman tuck us the trip:
And Marshall and me's in pardnership!

DOT LEEDLE BOY

OT'S a leedle Gristmas story
　　Dot I told der leedle folks—
Und I vant you stop dot laughin'
　　Und grackin' funny jokes!—
So help me Peter-Moses!
　　Ot's no time for monkey-shine,
Ober I vast told you somedings
　　Of dot leedle boy of mine!

Ot vas von cold Vinter vedder,
　　Ven der snow vas all about—
Dot you have to chop der hatchet
　　Eef you got der sauerkraut!
Und der cheekens on der hind leg
　　Vas standin' in der shine
Der sun shmile out dot morning
　　On dot leedle boy of mine.

He vas yoost a leedle baby
　　Not bigger as a doll
Dot time I got acquaintet—
　　Ach! you ought to heard 'im squall!—

I grackys! dot's der moosic
  Ot make me feel so fine
Ven first I vas been marriet—
  Oh, dot leedle boy of mine!

He look yoost like his fader!—
  So, ven der vimmen said,
"Vot a purty leedle baby!"
  Katrina shake der head. . . .
I dink she must 'a' notice
  Dot der baby vas a-gryin',
Und she cover up der blankets
  Of dot leedle boy of mine.

Vel, ven he vas got bigger,
  Dot he grawl und bump his nose,
Und make der table over,
  Und molasses on his glothes—
Dot make 'im all der sveeter,—
  So I say to my Katrine,
"Better you vas quit a-shpankin'
  Dot leedle boy of mine!"

No more he vas older
  As about a dozen months
He speak der English language
  Und der German—bote at vonce!
Und he dringk his glass of lager
  Like a Londsman fon der Rhine—
Und I klingk my glass togeder
  Mit dot leedle boy of mine!

I vish you could 'a' seen id—
   Ven he glimb up on der chair
Und shmash der lookin'-glasses
   Ven he try to comb his hair
Mit a hammer!—Und Katrina
   Say, "Dot's an ugly sign!"
But I laugh und vink my fingers
   At dot leedle boy of mine.

But vonce, dot Vinter morning,
   He shlip out in der snow
Mitout no stockin's on 'im.—
   He say he "vant to go
Und fly some mit der birdies!"
   Und ve give 'im medi-cine
Ven he catch der "parrygoric"—
   Dot leedle boy of mine!

Und so I set und nurse 'im,
   Vile der Gristmas vas come roun',
Und I told 'im 'bout "Kriss Kringle,"
   How he come der chimbly down:
Und I ask 'im eef he love 'im
   Eef he bring 'im someding fine?
"Nicht besser as mein fader,"
   Say dot leedle boy of mine.—

Und he put his arms aroun' me
   Und hug so close und tight,
I hear der gclock a-tickin'
   All der balance of der night! . . .

Someding make me feel so funny
  Ven I say to my Katrine,
"Let us go und fill der stockin's
  Of dot leedle boy of mine."

Vell.—Ve buyed a leedle horses
  Dot you pull 'im mit a shtring,
Und a leedle fancy jay-bird—
  Eef you vant to hear 'im sing
You took 'im by der topknot
  Und yoost blow in behine—
Und dot make much *spectakel*
  For dot leedle boy of mine!

Und gandies, nuts und raizens—
  Und I buy a leedle drum
Dot I vant to hear 'im rattle
  Ven der Gristmas morning come!
Und a leedle shmall tin rooster
  Dot vould crow so loud und fine
Ven he sqveeze 'im in der morning,
  Dot leedle boy of mine!

Und—vile ve vas a-fixin'—
  Dot leedle boy vake out!
I t'ought he been a-dreamin'
  "Kriss Kringle" vas about,—
For he say—*"Dot's him!—I see 'im
  Mit der shtars dot make der shine!"*
Und he yoost keep on a-gryin'—
  Dot leedle boy of mine,—

Und gottin' vorse und vorser—
  Und tumble on der bed!
So—ven der doctor seen id,
  He kindo' shake his head,
Und feel his pulse—und visper,
  "Der boy is a-dyin'."
You dink I could *believe* id?—
  Dot leedle boy of mine?

I told you, friends—dot's someding,
  Der last time dot he speak
Und say, *"Goot-by, Kriss Kringle!"*
  —Dot make me feel so veak
I yoost kneel down und drimble,
  Und bur-sed out a-gryin',
"Mein Gott, mein Gott in Himmel!—
  Dot leedle boy of mine!"

          .   .   .   .   .   .

Der sun don't shine *dot* Gristmas!
  . . . Eef dot leedle boy vould *liff'd*—
No deefer-en'! for *Heaven* vas
  His leedle Gristmas gift!
Und der *rooster,* und der *gandy,*
  Und me—und my Katrine—
Und der jay-bird—is a-vaiting
  For dot leedle boy of mine.

I SMOKE MY PIPE

I CAN'T extend to every friend
  In need a helping hand—
No matter though I wish it so,
  'Tis not as Fortune planned;
But haply may I fancy they
  Are men of different stripe
Than others think who hint and wink,—
  And so—I smoke my pipe!

A golden coal to crown the bowl—
  My pipe and I alone,—
I sit and muse with idler views
  Perchance than I should own:—
It might be worse to own the purse
  Whose glutted bowels gripe
In little qualms of stinted alms;
  And so I smoke my pipe.

And if inclined to moor my mind
  And cast the anchor Hope,
A puff of breath will put to death
  The morbid misanthrope

That lurks inside—as errors hide
  In standing forms of type
To mar at birth some line of worth;
  And so I smoke my pipe.

The subtle stings misfortune flings
  Can give me little pain
When my narcotic spell has wrought
  This quiet in my brain:
When I can waste the past in taste
  So luscious and so ripe
That like an elf I hug myself;
  And so I smoke my pipe.

And wrapped in shrouds of drifting clouds
  I watch the phantom's flight,
Till alien eyes from Paradise
  Smile on me as I write:
And I forgive the wrongs that live,
  As lightly as I wipe
Away the tear that rises here;
  And so I smoke my pipe.

RED RIDING-HOOD

SWEET little myth of the nursery story—
  Earliest love of mine infantile breast,
Be something tangible, bloom in thy glory
  Into existence, as thou art addressed!
Hasten! appear to me, guileless and good—
Thou are so dear to me, Red Riding-Hood!

Azure-blue eyes, in a marvel of wonder,
  Over the dawn of a blush breaking out;
Sensitive nose, with a little smile under
  Trying to hide in a blossoming pout—
Couldn't be serious, try as you would,
Little mysterious Red Riding-Hood!

Hah! little girl, it is desolate, lonely,
  Out in this gloomy old forest of Life!—
Here are not pansies and buttercups only—
  Brambles and briers as keen as a knife;
And a Heart, ravenous, trails in the wood
  For the meal have he must,—Red Riding-
    Hood!

IF I KNEW WHAT POETS KNOW

IF I knew what poets know,
    Would I write a rhyme
Of the buds that never blow
    In the summer-time?
Would I sing of golden seeds
Springing up in ironweeds?
And of rain-drops turned to snow,
If I knew what poets know?

Did I know what poets do,
    .Would I sing a song
Sadder than the pigeon's coo
    When the days are long?
Where I found a heart in pain,
I would make it glad again;
And the false should be the true,
Did I know what poets do.

If I knew what poets know,
    I would find a theme
Sweeter than the placid flow
    Of the fairest dream:
I would sing of love that lives
On the errors it forgives;
And the world would better grow
If I knew what poets know.

AN OLD SWEETHEART OF MINE

AN old sweetheart of mine!—Is this her presence
here with me,
Or but a vain creation of a lover's memory?
A fair, illusive vision that would vanish into air
Dared I even touch the silence with the whisper of
a prayer?

Nay, let me then believe in all the blended false and
true—
The semblance of the *old* love and the substance of
the *new,*—
The *then* of changeless sunny days—the *now* of
shower and shine—
But Love forever smiling—as that old sweetheart
of mine.

This ever-restful sense of *home,* though shouts ring
in the hall.—
The easy chair—the old book-shelves and prints
along the wall;
The rare *Habanas* in their box, or gaunt church-
warden-stem
That often wags, above the jar, derisively at them.

As one who cons at evening o'er an album, all alone,
And muses on the faces of the friends that he has
known,

"So I turn the leaves of Fancy, till, in shadowy design,
   I find the smiling features of an old sweetheart of mine"

So I turn the leaves of Fancy, till, in shadowy de-
    sign,
I find the smiling features of an old sweetheart of
    mine.

The lamplight seems to glimmer with a flicker of
    surprise,
As I turn it low—to rest me of the dazzle in my
    eyes,
And light my pipe in silence, save a sigh that seems
    to yoke
Its fate with my tobacco and to vanish with the
    smoke.

'Tis a *fragrant* retrospection,—for the loving
    thoughts that start
Into being are like perfume from the blossom of the
    heart;
And to dream the old dreams over is a luxury di-
    vine—
When my truant fancies wander with that old
    sweetheart of mine.

Though I hear beneath my study, like a fluttering of
    wings,
The voices of my children and the mother as she
    sings—
I feel no twinge of conscience to deny me any
    theme
When Care has cast her anchor in the harbor of a
    dream—

In fact, to speak in earnest, I believe it adds a
    charm
To spice the good a trifle with a little dust of
    harm,—
For I find an extra flavor in Memory's mellow
    wine
That makes me drink the deeper to that old sweet-
    heart of mine

O Childhood-days enchanted; O the magic of the
    Spring!—
With all green boughs to blossom white, and all
    bluebirds to sing!
When all the air, to toss and quaff, made life a
    jubilee
And changed the children's song and laugh to
    shrieks of ecstasy.

With eyes half closed in clouds that ooze from lips
    that taste, as well,
The peppermint and cinnamon, I hear the old
    School bell,
And from "Recess" romp in again from "Black-
    man's" broken line,
To smile, behind my "lesson," at that old sweet-
    heart of mine.

A face of lily-beauty, with a form of airy grace,
Floats out of my tobacco as the Genii from the vase;

And I thrill beneath the glances of a pair of azure
eyes
As glowing as the summer and as tender as the
skies.

I can see the pink sunbonnet and the little checkered
dress
She wore when first I kissed her and she answered
the caress
With the written declaration that, "as surely as the
vine
Grew 'round the stump," she loved me—that old
sweetheart of mine.

Again I made her presents, in a really helpless
way,—
The big "Rhode Island Greening"—I was hungry,
too, that day!—
But I followed her from Spelling, with her hand behind her—so—
And I slip the apple in it—and the Teacher doesn't
know!

I give my *treasures* to her—all,—my pencil—blue-
and-red;—
And, if little girls played marbles, *mine* should all
be *hers,* instead!
But *she* gave me her *photograph,* and printed "Ever
Thine"
Across the back—in blue-and-red—that old sweet-
heart of mine!

And again I feel the pressure of her slender little
 hand,
As we used to talk together of the future we had
 planned,—
When I should be a poet, and with nothing else
 to do
But write the tender verses that she set the music
 to . . .

When we should live together in a cozy little cot
Hid in a nest of roses, with a fairy garden-spot,
Where the vines were ever fruited, and the weather
 ever fine,
And the birds were ever singing for that old sweet-
 heart of mine.

When I should be her lover forever and a day,
And she my faithful sweetheart till the golden hair
 was gray;
And we should be so happy that when either's lips
 were dumb
They would not smile in Heaven till the other's kiss
 had come.

But, ah! my dream is broken by a step upon the
 stair,
And the door is softly opened, and—my wife is
 standing there:
Yet with eagerness and rapture all my visions I
 resign,—
To greet the *living* presence of that old sweetheart
 of mine.

SQUIRE HAWKINS'S STORY

I HAIN'T no hand at tellin' tales,
Er spinnin' yarns, as the sailors say;
Someway o' 'nother, language fails
To slide fer me in the oily way
That *lawyers* has; and I wisht it would,
Fer I've got somepin' that I call good;
But bein' only a country squire,
I've learned to listen and admire,
Ruther preferrin' to be addressed
Than talk myse'f—but I'll do my best:—

Old Jeff Thompson—well, I'll say,
Was the clos'test man I ever saw!—
Rich as cream, but the porest pay,
And the meanest man to work fer—La!
I've knowed that man to work one "hand"—
Fer little er nothin', you understand—
From four o'clock in the morning light
Tel eight and nine o'clock at night,
And then find fault with his appetite!
He'd drive all over the neighberhood

To miss the place where a toll-gate stood,
And slip in town, by some old road
That no two men in the county knowed,
With a jag o' wood, and a sack o' wheat.
That wouldn't burn and you couldn't eat!
And the trades he'd make, 'll I jest de-clare,
Was enough to make a preacher swear!
And then he'd hitch, and hang about
Tel the lights in the toll-gate was blowed out,
And then the turnpike he'd turn in
And sneak his way back home ag'in!

Some folks hint, and I make no doubt.
That that's what wore his old wife out—
Toilin' away from day to day
And year to year, through heat and cold,
Uncomplainin'—the same old way
The martyrs died in the days of old;
And a-clingin', too, as the martyrs done,
To one fixed faith, and her *only* one,—
Little Patience, the sweetest child
That ever wept unrickonciled,
Er felt the pain and the ache and sting
That only a mother's death can bring.

Patience Thompson!—I think that name
Must 'a' come from a power above,
Fer it seemed to fit her jest the same
As a *gaiter* would, er a fine kid glove!
And to see that girl, with all the care

Of the household on her—I de-clare
It was *oudacious,* the work she'd do,
And the thousand plans that she'd putt
    through;
And sing like a medder-lark all day long,
And drowned her cares in the joys o' song;
And *laugh* sometimes tel the farmer's "hand,"
Away fur off in the fields, would stand
A-listenin', with the plow half drawn,
Tel the coaxin' echoes called him on;
And the furries seemed, in his dreamy eyes,
Like foot-paths a-leadin' to Paradise,
As off through the hazy atmosphere
The call fer dinner reached his ear.

Now *love's* as cunnin' a little thing
As a hummin'-bird upon the wing,
And as liable to poke his nose
Jest where folks would least suppose,—
And more'n likely build his nest
Right in the heart you'd leave unguessed,
And live and thrive at your expense—
At least, that's *my* experience.
And old Jeff Thompson often thought,
In his se'fish way, that the quiet John
Was a stiddy chap, as a farm-hand *ought*
To always be,—fer the airliest dawn
Found John busy—and "*easy,*" too,
Whenever his *wages* would fall due!—
To sum him up with a final touch,

He *eat* so little and *worked* so much,
That old Jeff laughed to hisse'f and said,
"He makes *me* money and airns his bread!"

But John, fer all of his quietude,
Would sometimes drap a word er so
That none but *Patience* understood,
And none but her was *meant* to know!—
Maybe at meal-times John would say,
As the sugar-bowl come down his way,
"Thanky, no; *my* coffee's sweet
Enough fer *me!*" with sich conceit,
She'd know at once, without no doubt,
He meant because *she* poured it out;
And smile and blush, and all sich stuff,
And ast ef it was *"strong* enough?"
And git the answer, neat and trim,
"It *couldn't* be too 'strong' fer *him!*"

And so things went fer 'bout a year,
Tel John, at last, found pluck to go
And pour his tale in the old man's ear—
And ef it had been *hot lead,* I know
It couldn't 'a' raised a louder fuss,
Ner 'a' riled the old man's temper wuss!
He jest *lit* in, and cussed and swore,
And lunged and rared, and ripped and tore,
And told John jest to leave his door,
And not to darken it no more!
But Patience cried, with eyes all wet,
"Remember, John, and don't ferget,

Whatever comes, I love you yet!"
But the old man thought, in his se'fish way,
"I'll see her married rich some day;
And *that,*" thinks he, "is money fer *me*—
And my will's *law,* as it ought to be!"

So when, in the course of a month er so,
A *widower,* with a farm er two,
Comes to Jeff's, w'y, the folks, you know,
Had to *talk*—as the folks'll do:
It was the talk of the neighberhood—
Patience and *John,* and *their* affairs;—
And this old chap with a few gray hairs
Had "cut John out," it was understood.
And some folks reckoned "Patience, too,
Knowed what *she* was a-goin' to do—
It was *like* her—la! indeed!—
All *she* loved was *dollars* and *cents*—
Like old *Jeff*—and they saw no need
Fer *John* to pine at *her* negligence!"

But others said, in a *kinder* way,
They missed the songs she used to sing—
They missed the smiles that used to play
Over her face, and the laughin' ring
Of her glad voice—that *every*thing
Of her *old* se'f seemed dead and gone,
And this was the ghost that they gazed on!

Tel finally it was noised about
There was a *weddin'* soon to be

Down at Jeff's; and the "cat was out"
Shore enough!—'Ll the *Jee-mun-nee!*
It *riled* me when John told me so,—
Fer *I was a friend o' John's,* you know;
And his trimblin' voice jest broke in two—
As a feller's voice'll sometimes do.—
And I says, says I, "Ef I know my biz—
And I think I know what *jestice* is,—
I've read *some* law—and I'd advise
A man like you to wipe his eyes
And square his jaws and start *ag'in,*
Fer jestice is a-goin' to win!"
And it wasn't long tel his eyes had cleared
As blue as the skies, and the *sun* appeared
In the shape of a good old-fashioned smile
That I hadn't seen fer a long, long while.

So we talked on fer a' hour er more,
And sunned ourselves in the open door,—
Tel a hoss-and-buggy down the road
Come a-drivin' up, that I guess John *knowed,*—
Fer he winked and says, "I'll dessappear—
They'd smell a mice ef they saw *me* here!"
And he thumbed his nose at the old gray mare,
And hid hisse'f in the house somewhere.

Well.—The rig drove up: and I raised my head
As old Jeff hollered to me and said
That "him and his old friend there had come
To see ef the squire was at home."
. . . I told 'em "I was; and I *aimed* to be

At every chance of a weddin'-fee!"
And then I laughed—and they laughed, too,—
Fer that was the object they had in view.
"Would I be on hands at eight that night?"
They ast; and 's-I, "You're mighty right,
I'll be on hand!" And then I *bu'st*
Out a-laughin' my very wu'st,—
And so did they, as they wheeled away
And drove to'rds town in a cloud o' dust.
Then I shet the door, and me and John
Laughed and *laughed,* and jest *laughed* on,
Tel Mother drapped her specs, and *by
Jeewhillikers!* I thought she'd *die!*—
And she couldn't 'a' told, I'll bet my hat,
What on earth she was laughin' at!

But all o' the fun o' the tale hain't done!—
Fer a drizzlin' rain had jest begun,
And a-havin' 'bout four mile' to ride,
I jest concluded I'd better light
Out fer Jeff's and save my hide,—
Fer *it was a-goin' to storm, that night!*
So we went down to the barn, and John
Saddled my beast, and I got on;
And he told me somepin' to not ferget,
And when I left, he was *laughin'* yet.

And, 'proachin' on to my journey's end,
The great big draps o' the rain come down,
And the thunder growled in a way to lend

An awful look to the lowerin' frown
The dull sky wore; and the lightnin' glanced
Tel my old mare jest *more'n* pranced,
And tossed her head, and bugged her eyes
To about four times their natchural size,
As the big black lips of the clouds 'ud drap
Out some oath of a thunderclap,
And threaten on in an undertone
That chilled a feller clean to the bone!

But I struck shelter soon enough
To save myse'f. And the house was jammed
With the women-folks, and the weddin'-
    stuff:—
A great, long table, fairly *crammed*
With big pound-cakes—and chops and steaks—
And roasts and stews—and stumick-aches
Of every fashion, form, and size,
From twisters up to punkin-pies!
And candies, oranges, and figs,
And reezins,—all the "whilligigs"
And "jim-cracks" that the law allows
On sich occasions!—Bobs and bows
Of gigglin' girls, with corkscrew curls,
And fancy ribbons, reds and blues,
And "beau-ketchers" and "curliques"
To beat the world! And seven o'clock
Brought old Jeff;—and brought—*the groom,*—
With a sideboard-collar on, and stock
That choked him so, he hadn't room
To *swaller* in, er even sneeze,

Er clear his th'oat with any ease
Er comfort—and a good square cough
Would saw his Adam's apple off!

But as fer *Patience—My!* Oomh-*oomh!—*
I never saw her look so sweet!—
Her face was cream and roses, too;
And then them eyes o' heavenly blue
Jest made an angel all complete!
And when she split 'em up in smiles
And splintered 'em around the room,
And danced acrost and met the groom,
And *laughed out loud*—It kind o' spiles
My language when I come to that—
Fer, as she laid away his hat,
Thinks I, *"The papers hid inside*
Of that said hat must make a bride
A happy one fer all her life,
Er else a *wrecked* and *wretched wife!"*
And, someway, then, I thought of *John,—*
Then looked towards *Patience.* . . . She was
    gone!—
The door stood open, and the rain
Was dashin' in; and sharp and plain
Above the storm we heerd a cry—
A ringin', laughin', loud "Good-by!"
That died away, as fleet and fast
A hoss's hoofs went splashin' past!
And that was all. 'Twas done that quick! . . .
You've heerd o' fellers "lookin' sick"?
I wisht you'd seen *the groom* jest then—

A—8

I wisht you'd seen them two old men,
With starin' eyes that fairly *glared*
At one another, and the scared
And empty faces of the crowd,—
I wisht you could 'a' been allowed
To jest look on and see it all,—
And heerd the girls and women bawl
And wring their hands; and heerd old Jeff
A-cussin' as he swung hisse'f
Upon his hoss, who champed his bit
As though old Nick had holt of it:
And cheek by jowl the two old wrecks
Rode off as though they'd break their necks.

And as we all stood starin' out
Into the night, I felt the brush
Of some one's hand, and turned about,
And heerd a voice that whispered, *"Hush!—-
They're waitin' in the kitchen, and
You're wanted. Don't you understand?"*
Well, ef my *memory* serves me now,
I think I winked.—Well, anyhow,
I left the crowd a-gawkin' there,
And jest slipped off around to where
The back door opened, and went in,
And turned and shet the door ag'in,
And maybe *locked* it—couldn't swear,—
A woman's arms around me makes
Me liable to make mistakes.—
I read a marriage license nex',
But as I didn't have my specs

I jest *inferred* it was all right,
And tied the knot so mortal-tight
That Patience and my old friend John
Was safe enough from that time on!

Well, now, I might go on and tell
How all the joke at last leaked out,
And how the youngsters raised the yell
And rode the happy groom about
Upon their shoulders; how the bride
Was kissed a hunderd times beside
The one *I* give her,—tel she cried
And laughed untel she like to died!
I might go on and tell you all
About the supper—and the *ball.*—
You'd ought to see me twist my heel
Through jest one old Furginny reel
Afore you die! er tromp the strings
Of some old fiddle tel she sings
Some old cowtillion, don't you know,
That putts the devil in yer toe!

We kep' the dancin' up tel *four*
O'clock, I reckon—maybe more.—
We hardly heerd the thunders roar,
Er *thought* about the *storm* that blowed—
And them two fellers on the road!
Tel all at onc't we heerd the door
Bu'st open, and a voice that *swore,*—
And old Jeff Thompson tuck the floor.
He shuck hisse'f and looked around

Like some old dog about half-drowned—
His hat, I reckon, *weighed ten pound*
To say the least, and I'll say, *shore,*
His *overcoat weighed fifty* more—
The wettest man you ever saw,
To have so dry a son-in-law!

He sized it all; and Patience laid
Her hand in John's, and looked afraid,
And waited. And a stiller set
O' folks, I *know,* you never met
In any court room, where with dread
They wait to hear a verdick read.

The old man turned his eyes on me:
"And have you married 'em?" says he.
I nodded "Yes." "Well, that'll do,"
He says, "and now we're th'ough with *you,*—
You jest clear out, and I decide
And promise to be satisfied!"
He hadn't nothin' more to say.
I saw, of course, how matters lay,
And left. But as I rode away
I heerd the roosters crow fer day.

A COUNTRY PATHWAY

I COME upon it suddenly, alone—
   A little pathway winding in the weeds
That fringe the roadside; and with dreams my own,
   I wander as it leads.

Full wistfully along the slender way,
   Through summer tan of freckled shade and shine,
I take the path that leads me as it may—
   Its every choice is mine.

A chipmunk, or a sudden-whirring quail,
   Is startled by my step as on I fare—
A garter-snake across the dusty trail
   Glances and—is not there.

Above the arching jimson-weeds flare twos
   And twos of sallow-yellow butterflies,
Like blooms of lorn primroses blowing loose
   When autumn winds arise.

The trail dips—dwindles—broadens then, and lifts
   Itself astride a cross-road dubiously,
And, from the fennel marge beyond it, drifts
   Still onward, beckoning me.

And though it needs must lure me mile on mile
　Out of the public highway, still I go,
My thoughts, far in advance in Indian file,
　Allure me even so.

Why, I am as a long-lost boy that went
　At dusk to bring the cattle to the bars,
And was not found again, though Heaven lent
　His mother all the stars

With which to seek him through that awful night.
　O years of nights as vain!—Stars never rise
But well might miss their glitter in the light
　Of tears in mother-eyes!

So—on, with quickened breaths, I follow still—
　My avant-courier must be obeyed!
Thus am I led, and thus the path, at will,
　Invites me to invade

A meadow's precincts, where my daring guide
　Clambers the steps of an old-fashioned stile,
And stumbles down again, the other side,
　To gambol there a while.

In pranks of hide-and-seek, as on ahead
　I see it running, while the clover-stalks
Shake rosy fists at me, as though they said—
　"You dog our country walks

"And mutilate us with your walking-stick!—
  We will not suffer tamely what you do,
And warn you at your peril,—for we'll sick
  Our bumblebees on you!"

But I smile back, in airy nonchalance,—
  The more determined on my wayward quest,
As some bright memory a moment dawns
  A morning in my breast—

Sending a thrill that hurries me along
  In faulty similes of childish skips,
Enthused with lithe contortions of a song
  Performing on my lips.

In wild meanderings o'er pasture wealth—
  Erratic wanderings through dead'ning lands,
Where sly old brambles, plucking me by stealth,
  Put berries in my hands:

Or the path climbs a boulder—wades a slough—
  Or, rollicking through buttercups and flags,
Goes gaily dancing o'er a deep bayou
  On old tree-trunks and snags:

Or, at the creek, leads o'er a limpid pool
  Upon a bridge the stream itself has made,
With some Spring-freshet for the mighty tool
  That its foundation laid.

I pause a moment here to bend and muse,
  With dreamy eyes, on my reflection, where
A boat-backed bug drifts on a helpless cruise,
  Or wildly oars the air,

As, dimly seen, the pirate of the brook—
  The pike, whose jaunty hulk denotes his speed—
Swings pivoting about, with wary look
  Of low and cunning greed.

Till, filled with other thought, I turn again
  To where the pathway enters in a realm
Of lordly woodland, under sovereign reign
  Of towering oak and elm.

A puritanic quiet here reviles
  The almost whispered warble from the hedge,
And takes a locust's rasping voice and files
  The silence to an edge.

In such a solitude my somber way
  Strays like a misanthrope within a gloom
Of his own shadows—till the perfect day
  Bursts into sudden bloom,

And crowns a long, declining stretch of space,
  Where King Corn's armies lie with flags unfurled,
And where the valley's dint in Nature's face
  Dimples a smiling world.

And lo! through mists that may not be dispelled,
 I see an old farm homestead, as in dreams,
Where, like a gem in costly setting held,
 The old log cabin gleams.

. . . .

O darling Pathway! lead me bravely on
 Adown your valley-way, and run before
Among the roses crowding up the lawn
 And thronging at the door,—

And carry up the echo there that shall
 Arouse the drowsy dog, that he may bay
The household out to greet the prodigal
 That wanders home to-day.

THE OLD GUITAR

NEGLECTED now is the old guitar
  And moldering into decay;
Fretted with many a rift and scar
  That the dull dust hides away,
While the spider spins a silver star
  In its silent lips to-day.

The keys hold only nerveless strings—
  The sinews of brave old airs
Are pulseless now; and the scarf that clings
  So closely here declares
A sad regret in its ravelings
  And the faded hue it wears.

But the old guitar, with a lenient grace,
  Has cherished a smile for me;
And its features hint of a fairer face
  That comes with a memory
Of a flower-and-perfume-haunted place
  And a moonlit balcony.

112

Music sweeter than words confess,
  Or the minstrel's powers invent,
Thrilled here once at the light caress
  Of the fairy hands that lent
This excuse for the kiss I press
  On the dear old instrument.

The rose of pearl with the jeweled stem
  Still blooms; and the tiny sets
In the circle all are here; the gem
  In the keys, and the silver frets;
But the dainty fingers that danced o'er them—
  Alas for the heart's regrets!—

Alas for the loosened strings to-day,
  And the wounds of rift and scar
On a worn old heart, with its roundelay
  Enthralled with a stronger bar
That Fate weaves on, through a dull decay
  Like that of the old guitar!

"FRIDAY AFTERNOON"

TO WILLIAM MORRIS PIERSON

[1868-1870]

OF the wealth of facts and fancies
　　That our memories may recall,
The old school-day romances
　　Are the dearest, after all!—
When some sweet thought revises
　　The half-forgotten tune
That opened "Exercises"
　　On "Friday Afternoon."

We seem to hear the clicking
　　Of the pencil and the pen,
And the solemn, ceaseless ticking
　　Of the timepiece ticking then;
And we note the watchful master,
　　As he waves the warning rod,
With our own heart beating faster
　　Than the boy's who threw the wad.

114

Some little hand uplifted,
  And the creaking of a shoe :—
A problem left unsifted
  For the teacher's hand to do:
The murmured hum of learning—
  And the flutter of a book;
The smell of something burning,
  And the school's inquiring look.

The bashful boy in blushes;
  And the girl, with glancing eyes,
Who hides her smiles, and hushes
  The laugh about to rise,—
Then, with a quick invention,
  Assumes a serious face,
To meet the words, "Attention!
  Every scholar in his place!"

The opening song, page 20.—
  Ah! dear old "Golden Wreath,"
You willed your sweets in plenty;
  And some who look beneath
The leaves of Time will linger,
  And loving tears will start,
As Fancy trails her finger
  O'er the index of the heart.

"Good News from Home"—We hear it
  Welling tremulous, yet clear
And holy as the spirit
  Of the song we used to hear—

"Good news for me"—(A throbbing
  And an aching melody)—
"Has come across the"—(sobbing,
  Yea, and salty) "dark blue sea!"

Or the pæan "Scotland's burning!"
  With its mighty surge and swell
Of chorus, still returning
  To its universal yell—
Till we're almost glad to drop to
  Something sad and full of pain—
And "Skip verse three," and stop, too,
  Ere our hearts are broke again.

Then "the big girls'" compositions,
  With their doubt, and hope, and glow
Of heart and face,—conditions
  Of "the big boys"—even so,—
When themes of "Spring," and "Summer"
  And of "Fall," and "Winter-time"
Droop our heads and hold us dumber
  Than the sleigh-bell's fancied chime.

Elocutionary science—
  (Still in changeless infancy!)—
With its "Cataline's Defiance,"
  And "The Banner of the Free":
Or, lured from Grandma's attic,
  A ramshackle "rocker" there,
Adds a skreek of the dramatic
  To the poet's "Old Arm-Chair."

Or the "Speech of Logan" shifts us
  From the pathos, to the fire;
And Tell (with Gessler) lifts us
  Many noble notches higher.—
Till a youngster, far from sunny,
  With sad eyes of watery blue,
Winds up with something "funny,"
  Like "Cock-a-doodle-do!"

Then a dialogue—selected
  For its realistic worth:—
The Cruel Boy detected
  With a turtle turned to earth
Back downward; and, in pleading,
  The Good Boy—strangely gay
At such a sad proceeding—
  Says, "Turn him over, pray!"

So the exercises taper
  Through gradations of delight
To the reading of "The Paper,"
  Which is entertaining—quite!
For it goes ahead and mentions
  "If a certain Mr. O.
Has serious intentions
  That he ought to tell her so."

It also "Asks permission
  To intimate to 'John'
The dubious condition
  Of the ground he's standing on":

And, dropping the suggestion
  To "mind what he's about,"
It stuns him with the question:
  "Does his mother know he's out?"

And among the contributions
  To this "Academic Press"
Are "Versified Effusions"
  By—"Our lady editress"—
Which fact is proudly stated
  By the *Chief* of the concern,—
"Though the verse communicated
  Bears the pen-name 'Fanny Fern.'

.   .   .   .   .

When all has been recited,
  And the teacher's bell is heard,
And visitors, invited,
  Have dropped a kindly word,
A hush of holy feeling
  Falls down upon us there,
As though the day were kneeling,
  With the twilight for the prayer.

.   .   .   .   .

Midst the wealth of facts and fancies
  That our memories may recall,
Thus the old school-day romances
  Are the dearest, after all!—
When some sweet thought revises
  The half-forgotten tune
That opened "Exercises,"
  On "Friday Afternoon."

"JOHNSON'S BOY"

THE world is turned ag'in' me,
  And people says, "They guess
That nothin' else is in me
  But pure maliciousness!"
I git the blame for doin'
  What other chaps destroy,
And I'm a-goin' to ruin
  Because I'm "Johnson's boy."

That ain't my *name*—I'd ruther
  They'd call me *Ike* or *Pat*—
But they've forgot the other—
  And so have *I*, for that!
I reckon it's as handy,
  When Nibsy breaks his toy,
Or some one steals his candy,
  To say 'twas *"Johnson's boy!"*

You can't git any water
  At the pump, and find the spout
So durn chuck-full o' mortar
  That you have to bore it out;

You tackle any scholar
  In Wisdom's wise employ,
And I'll bet you half a dollar
  He'll say it's "Johnson's boy!"

Folks don't know how I suffer
  In my uncomplainin' way—
They think I'm gittin' tougher
  And tougher every day.
Last Sunday night, when Flinder
  Was a-shoutin' out for joy,
And some one shook the winder,
  He prayed for "Johnson's boy."

I'm tired of bein' follered
  By farmers every day,
And then o' bein' collared
  For coaxin' hounds away;
Hounds always plays me double—
  It's a trick they all enjoy—
To git me into trouble,
  Because I'm "Johnson's boy."

But if I git to Heaven,
  I hope the Lord'll see
Some boy has been perfect,
  And lay it on to me;
. I'll swell the song sonorous,
  And clap my wings for joy,
And sail off on the chorus—
  "Hurrah for 'Johnson's boy!'"

HER BEAUTIFUL HANDS

O YOUR hands—they are strangely fair!
Fair—for the jewels that sparkle there,—
Fair—for the witchery of the spell
That ivory keys alone can tell;
But when their delicate touches rest
Here in my own do I love them best,
As I clasp with eager, acquisitive spans
My glorious treasure of beautiful hands!

Marvelous—wonderful—beautiful hands!
They can coax roses to bloom in the strands
Of your brown tresses; and ribbons will twine,
Under mysterious touches of thine,
Into such knots as entangle the soul
And fetter the heart under such a control
As only the strength of my love understands—
My passionate love for your beautiful hands.

As I remember the first fair touch
Of those beautiful hands that I love so much,
I seem to thrill as I then was thrilled,
Kissing the glove that I found unfilled—
When I met your gaze, and the queenly bow,

As you said to me, laughingly, "Keep it
  now!" . . .
And dazed and alone in a dream I stand,
Kissing this ghost of your beautiful hand.

When first I loved, in the long ago,
And held your hand as I told you so—
Pressed and caressed it and gave it a kiss
And said "I could die for a hand like this!"
Little I dreamed love's fullness yet
Had to ripen when eyes were wet
And prayers were vain in their wild demands
For one warm touch of your beautiful hands.

.   .   .   .

Beautiful Hands!—O Beautiful Hands!
Could you reach out of the alien lands
Where you are lingering, and give me, to-night,
Only a touch—were it ever so light—
My heart were soothed, and my weary brain
Would lull itself into rest again;
For there is no solace the world commands
Like the caress of your beautiful hands.

NATURAL PERVERSITIES

I AM not prone to moralize
  In scientific doubt
On certain facts that Nature tries
  To puzzle us about,—
For I am no philosopher
  Of wise elucidation,
But speak of things as they occur,
  From simple observation.

I notice *little* things—to wit :—
  I never missed a train
Because I didn't *run* for it ;
  I never knew it rain
That my umbrella wasn't lent,—
  Or, when in my possession,
The sun but wore, to all intent,
  A jocular expression.

I never knew a creditor
  To dun me for a debt
But I was "cramped" or "bu'sted"; or
  I never knew one yet,

123

When I had plenty in my purse,
  To make the least invasion,—
As I, accordingly perverse,
  Have courted no occasion.

Nor do I claim to comprehend
  What Nature has in view
In giving us the very friend
  To trust we oughtn't to.—
But so it is: The trusty gun
  Disastrously exploded
Is always sure to be the one
  We didn't think was loaded.

Our moaning is another's mirth,—
  And what is worse by half,
We say the funniest thing on earth
  And never raise a laugh:
'Mid friends that love us over well,
  And sparkling jests and liquor,
Our hearts somehow are liable
  To melt in tears the quicker.

We reach the wrong when most we seek
  The right; in like effect,
We stay the strong and not the weak—
  Do most when we neglect.—
Neglected genius—truth be said—
  As wild and quick as tinder,
The more you seek to help ahead
  The more you seem to hinder.

I've known the least the greatest, too—
   And, on the selfsame plan,
The biggest fool I ever knew
   Was quite a little man:
We find we ought, and then we won't—
   We prove a thing, then doubt it,—
Know *everything* but when we don't
   Know *anything* about it.

THE SILENT VICTORS

MAY 30, 1878

Dying for victory, cheer on cheer
Thundered on his eager ear.
          —CHARLES L. HOLSTEIN.

I

DEEP, tender, firm and true, the Nation's heart
     Throbs for her gallant heroes passed away,
Who in grim Battle's drama played their part,
     And slumber here to-day.—

Warm hearts that beat their lives out at the shrine
     Of Freedom, while our country held its breath
As brave battalions wheeled themselves in line
     And marched upon their death:

When Freedom's Flag, its natal wounds scarce
          healed,
     Was torn from peaceful winds and flung again
To shudder in the storm of battle-field—
     The elements of men,—

When every star that glittered was a mark
     For Treason's ball, and every rippling bar
Of red and white was sullied with the dark
     And purple stain of war:

126

'When angry guns, like famished beasts of prey,
  Were howling o'er their gory feast of lives,
And sending dismal echoes far away
  To mothers, maids, and wives:—

The mother, kneeling in the empty night,
  With pleading hands uplifted for the son
Who, even as she prayed, had fought the fight—
  The victory had won:

The wife, with trembling hand that wrote to say
  The babe was waiting for the sire's caress—
The letter meeting that upon the way,—
  The babe was fatherless:

The maiden, with her lips, in fancy, pressed
  Against the brow once dewy with her breath,
Now lying numb, unknown, and uncaressed
  Save by the dews of death.

II

What meed of tribute can the poet pay
  The Soldier, but to trail the ivy-vine
Of idle rhyme above his grave to-day
  In epitaph design?—

Or wreathe with laurel-words the icy brows
  That ache no longer with a dream of fame,
But, pillowed lowly in the narrow house,
  Renowned beyond the name.

The dewy tear-drops of the night may fall,
  And tender morning with her shining hand
May brush them from the grasses green and tall
  That undulate the land.—

Yet song of Peace nor din of toil and thrift,
  Nor chanted honors, with the flowers we heap,
Can yield us hope the Hero's head to lift
  Out of its dreamless sleep:

The dear old Flag, whose faintest flutter flies
  A stirring echo through each patriot breast,
Can never coax to life the folded eyes
  That saw its wrongs redressed—

That watched it waver when the fight was hot,
  And blazed with newer courage to its aid,
Regardless of the shower of shell and shot
  Through which the charge was made;—

And when, at last, they saw it plume its wings,
  Like some proud bird in stormy element,
And soar untrammeled on its wanderings,
  They closed in death, content.

III

O Mother, you who miss the smiling face
  Of that dear boy who vanished from your sight
And left you weeping o'er the vacant place
  He used to fill at night,—

Who left you dazed, bewildered, on a day
   That echoed wild huzzas, and roar of guns
That drowned the farewell words you tried to say
   To incoherent ones;—

Be glad and proud you had the life to give—
   Be comforted through all the years to come,—
Your country has a longer life to live,
   Your son a better home.

O Widow, weeping o'er the orphaned child,
   Who only lifts his questioning eyes to send
A keener pang to grief unreconciled,—
   Teach him to comprehend

He had a father brave enough to stand
   Before the fire of Treason's blazing gun,
That, dying, he might will the rich old land
   Of Freedom to his son.

And, Maiden, living on through lonely years
   In fealty to love's enduring ties,—
With strong faith gleaming through the tender
      tears
   That gather in your eyes,

Look up! and own, in gratefulness of prayer,
   Submission to the will of Heaven's High Host:—
I see your Angel-soldier pacing there,
   Expectant at his post.—

I see the rank and file of armies vast,
   That muster under one supreme control;
I hear the trumpet sound the signal-blast—
   The calling of the roll—

The grand divisions falling into line
   And forming, under voice of One alone
Who gives command, and joins with tongue divine
   The hymn that shakes the Throne.

IV

And thus, in tribute to the forms that rest
   In their last camping-ground, we strew the bloom
And fragrance of the flowers they loved the best,
   In silence o'er the tomb.

With reverent hands we twine the Hero's wreath
   And clasp it tenderly on stake or stone
That stands the sentinel for each beneath
   Whose glory is our own.

While in the violet that greets the sun,
   We see the azure eye of some lost boy;
And in the rose the ruddy cheek of one
   We kissed in childish joy,—

Recalling, haply, when he marched away,
   He laughed his loudest though his eyes were
      wet.—
The kiss he gave his mother's brow that day
   Is there and burning yet:

And through the storm of grief around her tossed,
  One ray of saddest comfort she may see,—
Four hundred thousand sons like hers were lost
  To weeping Liberty.

    .   .   .   .

But draw aside the drapery of gloom,
  And let the sunshine chase the clouds away
And gild with brighter glory every tomb
  We decorate to-day:

And in the holy silence reigning round,
  While prayers of perfume bless the atmosphere,
Where loyal souls of love and faith are found,
  Thank God that Peace is here!

And let each angry impulse that may start,
  Be smothered out of every loyal breast;
And, rocked within the cradle of the heart,
  Let every sorrow rest.

SCRAPS

THERE'S a habit I have nurtured,
    From the sentimental time
When my life was like a story,
    And my heart a happy rhyme,—
Of clipping from the paper,
    Or magazine, perhaps,
The idle songs of dreamers,
    Which I treasure as my scraps.

They hide among my letters,
    And they find a cozy nest
In the bosom of my wrapper,
    And the pockets of my vest;
They clamber in my fingers
    Till my dreams of wealth relapse
In fairer dreams than Fortune's
    Though I find them only scraps.

Sometimes I find, in tatters
    Like a beggar, form as fair
As ever gave to Heaven
    The treasure of a prayer;
And words all dim and faded,
    And obliterate in part,
Grow into fadeless meanings
    That are printed on the heart.

132

Sometimes a childish jingle
  Flings an echo, sweet and clear,
And thrills me as I listen
  To the laughs I used to hear;
And I catch the gleam of faces,
  And the glimmer of glad eyes
That peep at me expectant
  O'er the walls of Paradise.

O syllables of measure!
  Though you wheel yourselves in line,
And await the further order
  Of this eager voice of mine;
You are powerless to follow
  O'er the field my fancy maps,
So I lead you back to silence
  Feeling you are only scraps.

AUGUST

A DAY of torpor in the sullen heat
 Of Summer's passion: In the sluggish
  stream
The panting cattle lave their lazy feet,
 With drowsy eyes, and dream.

Long since the winds have died, and in the sky
 There lives no cloud to hint of Nature's
  grief;
The sun glares ever like an evil eye,
 And withers flower and leaf.

Upon the gleaming harvest-field remote
 The thresher lies deserted, like some old
Dismantled galleon that hangs afloat
 Upon a sea of gold.

The yearning cry of some bewildered bird
 Above an empty nest, and truant boys
Along the river's shady margin heard—
 A harmony of noise—

134

A melody of wrangling voices blent
 With liquid laughter, and with rippling calls
Of piping lips and thrilling echoes sent
 To mimic waterfalls.

And through the hazy veil the atmosphere
 Has draped about the gleaming face of Day,
The sifted glances of the sun appear
 In splinterings of spray.

The dusty highway, like a cloud of dawn,
 Trails o'er the hillside, and the passer-by,
A tired ghost in misty shroud, toils on
 His journey to the sky.

And down across the valley's drooping sweep,
 Withdrawn to farthest limit of the glade,
The forest stands in silence, drinking deep
 Its purple wine of shade.

The gossamer floats up on phantom wing;
 The sailor-vision voyages the skies
And carries into chaos everything
 That freights the weary eyes:

Till, throbbing on and on, the pulse of heat
 Increases—reaches—passes fever's height,
And Day sinks into slumber, cool and sweet,
 Within the arms of Night.

A—10

DEAD IN SIGHT OF FAME

DIED—*Early morning of September 5, 1876, and in the gleaming dawn of "name and fame," Hamilton J. Dunbar.*

D EAD! Dead! Dead!
   We thought him ours alone;
And were so proud to see him tread
The rounds of fame, and lift his head
   Where sunlight ever shone;
But now our aching eyes are dim,
And look through tears in vain for him.

Name! Name! Name!
   It was his diadem;
Nor ever tarnish-taint of shame
Could dim its luster—like a flame
   Reflected in a gem,
He wears it blazing on his brow
Within the courts of Heaven now.

Tears! Tears! Tears!
  Like dews upon the leaf
That bursts at last—from out the years
The blossom of a trust appears
  That blooms above the grief;
And mother, brother, wife and child
Will see it and be reconciled.

IN THE DARK

O IN the depths of midnight
    What fancies haunt the brain!
When even the sigh of the sleeper
    Sounds like a sob of pain.

A sense of awe and of wonder
    I may never well define,—
For the thoughts that come in the shadows
    Never come in the shine.

The old clock down in the parlor
    Like a sleepless mourner grieves,
And the seconds drip in the silence
    As the rain drips from the eaves.

And I think of the hands that signal
    The hours there in the gloom,
And wonder what angel watchers
    Wait in the darkened room.

And I think of the smiling faces
  That used to watch and wait,
Till the click of the clock was answered
  By the click of the opening gate.—

They are not there now in the evening—
  Morning or noon—not there;
Yet I know that they keep their vigil,
  And wait for me Somewhere.

THE IRON HORSE

NO song is mine of Arab steed—
  My courser is of nobler blood,
And cleaner limb and fleeter speed,
  And greater strength and hardihood
Than ever cantered wild and free
Across the plains of Araby.

Go search the level desert land
From Sana on to Samarcand—
Wherever Persian prince has been,
Or Dervish, Sheik, or Bedouin,
And I defy you there to point
  Me out a steed the half so fine—
From tip of ear to pastern-joint—
  As this old iron horse of mine.

You do not know what beauty is—
  You do not know what gentleness
  His answer is to my caress!—
Why, look upon this gait of his,—
A touch upon his iron rein—
  He moves with such a stately grace

The sunlight on his burnished mane
  Is barely shaken in its place;
  And at a touch he changes pace,
And, gliding backward, stops again.

And talk of mettle—Ah! my friend,
  Such passion smolders in his breast
That when awakened it will send
  A thrill of rapture wilder than
  E'er palpitated heart of man
  When flaming at its mightiest.
And there's a fierceness in his ire—
  And maddened majesty that leaps
Along his veins in blood of fire,
  Until the path his vision sweeps
Spins out behind him like a thread
  Unraveled from the reel of time,
  As, wheeling on his course sublime,
The earth revolves beneath his tread.

Then stretch away, my gallant steed!
  Thy mission is a noble one:
  Thou bear'st the father to the son,
And sweet relief to bitter need;
Thou bear'st the stranger to his friends;
  Thou bear'st the pilgrim to the shrine,
And back again the prayer he sends
  That God will prosper me and mine,—
The star that on thy forehead gleams
Has blossomed in our brightest dreams.

Then speed thee on thy glorious race!
The mother waits thy ringing pace;
The father leans an anxious ear
The thunder of thy hooves to hear;
The lover listens, far away,
To catch thy keen exultant neigh;
And, where thy breathings roll and rise,
The husband strains his eager eyes,
And laugh of wife and baby-glee
Ring out to greet and welcome thee.
Then stretch away! and when at last
  The master's hand shall gently check
Thy mighty speed, and hold thee fast,
  The world will pat thee on the neck.

DEAD LEAVES

DAWN

A S though a gipsy maiden with dim look,
　　Sat crooning by the roadside of the year,
So, Autumn, in thy strangeness, thou art here
To read dark fortunes for us from the book
Of fate; thou flingest in the crinkled brook
　　The trembling maple's gold, and frosty-clear
　　Thy mocking laughter thrills the atmosphere,
And drifting on its current calls the rook
To other lands. As one who wades, alone,
　　Deep in the dusk, and hears the minor talk
Of distant melody, and finds the tone,
　　In some weird way compelling him to stalk
The paths of childhood over,—so I moan,
　　And like a troubled sleeper, groping, walk.

DUSK

T HE frightened herds of clouds across the sky
　　Trample the sunshine down, and chase the
　　　　day
Into the dusky forest-lands of gray
And somber twilight. Far, and faint, and high

143

The wild goose trails his harrow, with a cry
   Sad as the wail of some poor castaway
   Who sees a vessel drifting far astray
Of his last hope, and lays him down to die.
The children, riotous from school, grow bold
   And quarrel with the wind, whose angry gust
Plucks off the summer hat, and flaps the fold
   Of many a crimson cloak, and twirls the dust
In spiral shapes grotesque, and dims the gold
   Of gleaming tresses with the blur of rust.

NIGHT

FUNEREAL Darkness, drear and desolate,
   Muffles the world. The moaning of the wind
   Is piteous with sobs of saddest kind;
And laughter is a phantom at the gate
Of memory. The long-neglected grate
   Within sprouts into flame and lights the mind
   With hopes and wishes long ago refined
To ashes,—long departed friends await
   Our words of welcome: and our lips are dumb
And powerless to greet the ones that press
   Old kisses there. The baby beats its drum,
And fancy marches to the dear caress
   Of mother-arms, and all the gleeful hum
Of home intrudes upon our loneliness.

OVER THE EYES OF GLADNESS

The voice of One hath spoken,
And the bended reed is bruised—
The golden bowl is broken,
And the silver cord is loosed.

OVER the eyes of gladness
   The lids of sorrow fall,
And the light of mirth is darkened
   Under the funeral pall.

The hearts that throbbed with rapture
   In dreams of the future years,
Are wakened from their slumbers,
   And their visions drowned in tears.

    .   .   .   .

Two buds on the bough in the morning—
   Twin buds in the smiling sun,
But the frost of death has fallen
   And blighted the bloom of one.

145

One leaf of life still folded
Has fallen from the stem,
Leaving the symbol teaching
There still are two of them,—

For though—through Time's gradations,
The *living* bud may burst,—
The *withered* one is gathered,
And blooms in Heaven first.

ONLY A DREAM

ONLY a dream!
        Her head is bent
Over the keys of the instrument,
While her trembling fingers go astray
In the foolish tune she tries to play.
He smiles in his heart, though his deep, sad
    eyes
Never change to a glad surprise
As he finds the answer he seeks confessed
In glowing features, and heaving breast.

Only a dream!
        Though the *fête* is grand,
And a hundred hearts at her command,
She takes no part, for her soul is sick
Of the Coquette's art and the Serpent's
    trick,—
She someway feels she would like to fling
Her sins away as a robe, and spring
Up like a lily pure and white,
And bloom alone for *him* to-night.

147

Only a dream
                    That the fancy weaves.
The lids unfold like the rose's leaves,
And the upraised eyes are moist and mild
As the prayerful eyes of a drowsy child.
Does she remember the spell they once
Wrought in the past a few short months?
Haply not—yet her lover's eyes
Never change to the glad surprise.

Only a dream!
                    He winds her form
Close in the coil of his curving arm,
And whirls her away in a gust of sound
As wild and sweet as the poets found
In the paradise where the silken tent
Of the Persian blooms in the Orient,—
While ever the chords of the music seem
Whispering sadly,—"Only a dream!"

"Only a dream that the fancy weaves"

OUR LITTLE GIRL

HER heart knew naught of sorrow,
  Nor the vaguest tint of sin—
'Twas an ever-blooming blossom
  Of the purity within:
And her hands knew only touches
  Of the mother's gentle care,
And the kisses and caresses
  Through the interludes of prayer.

Her baby-feet had journeyed
  Such a little distance here,
They could have found no briers
  In the path to interfere;
The little cross she carried
  Could not weary her, we know,
For it lay as lightly on her
  As a shadow on the snow.

And yet the way before us—
  O how empty now and drear!—
How ev'n the dews of roses
  Seem as dripping tears for her!
And the song-birds all seem crying,
  As the winds cry and the rain,
All sobbingly,—"We want—we want
  Our little girl again!"

THE FUNNY LITTLE FELLOW

'TWAS a Funny Little Fellow
   Of the very purest type,
For he had a heart as mellow
   As an apple over ripe;
And the brightest little twinkle
   When a funny thing occurred,
And the lightest little tinkle
   Of a laugh you ever heard!

His smile was like the glitter
   Of the sun in tropic lands,
And his talk a sweeter twitter
   Than the swallow understands;
Hear him sing—and tell a story—
   Snap a joke—ignite a pun,—
'Twas a capture—rapture—glory,
   An explosion—all in one!

Though he hadn't any money—
  That condiment which tends
To make a fellow "honey"
  For the palate of his friends;—
Sweet simples he compounded—
  Sovereign antidotes for sin
Or taint,—a faith unbounded
  That his friends were genuine.

He wasn't honored, maybe—
  For his songs of praise were slim,—
Yet I never knew a baby
  That wouldn't crow for him;
I never knew a mother
  But urged a kindly claim
Upon him as a brother,
  At the mention of his name.

The sick have ceased their sighing,
  And have even found the grace
Of a smile when they were dying
  As they looked upon his face;
And I've seen his eyes of laughter
  Melt in tears that only ran
As though, swift-dancing after,
  Came the Funny Little Man.

He laughed away the sorrow
  And he laughed away the gloom
We are all so prone to borrow
  From the darkness of the tomb;

A—11

And he laughed across the ocean
   Of a happy life, and passed,
With a laugh of glad emotion,
   Into Paradise at last.

And I think the Angels knew him,
   And had gathered to await
His coming, and run to him
   Through the widely opened Gate,
With their faces gleaming sunny
   For his laughter-loving sake,
And thinking, "What a funny
   Little Angel he will make!"

SONG OF THE NEW YEAR

I HEARD the bells at midnight
 Ring in the dawning year;
And above the clanging chorus
 Of the song, I seemed to hear
A choir of mystic voices
 Flinging echoes, ringing clear,
From a band of angels winging
 Through the haunted atmosphere:
    "Ring out the shame and sorrow,
     And the misery and sin,
    That the dawning of the morrow
    May in peace be ushered in."

And I thought of all the trials
 The departed years had cost,
And the blooming hopes and pleasures
 That are withered now and lost;
And with joy I drank the music
 Stealing o'er the feeling there
As the spirit song came pealing
 On the silence everywhere:
    "Ring out the shame and sorrow,
     And the misery and sin,
    That the dawning of the morrow
    May in peace be ushered in."

153

And I listened as a lover
　To an utterance that flows
In syllables like dewdrops
　From the red lips of a rose,
Till the anthem, fainter growing,
　Climbing higher, chiming on
Up the rounds of happy rhyming,
　Slowly vanished in the dawn:
　　　　　"Ring out the shame and sorrow,
　　　　　　And the misery and sin,
　　　　　That the dawning of the morrow
　　　　　　May in peace be ushered in."

Then I raised my eyes to Heaven,
　And with trembling lips I pled
For a blessing for the living
　And a pardon for the dead;
And like a ghost of music
　Slowly whispered—lowly sung—
Came the echo pure and holy
　In the happy angel tongue:
　　　　　"Ring out the shame and sorrow,
　　　　　　And the misery and sin,
　　　　　And the dawn of every morrow
　　　　　　Will in peace be ushered in."

A LETTER TO A FRIEND

THE past is like a story
　　I have listened to in dreams
That vanished in the glory
　　Of the Morning's early gleams;
And—at my shadow glancing—
　　I feel a loss of strength,
As the Day of Life advancing
　　Leaves it shorn of half its length.

But it's all in vain to worry
　　At the rapid race of Time—
And he flies in such a flurry
　　When I trip him with a rhyme,
I'll bother him no longer
　　Than to thank you for the thought
That "my fame is growing stronger
　　As you really think it ought."

And though I fall below it,
　　I might know as much of mirth
To live and die a poet
　　Of unacknowledged worth;
For Fame is but a vagrant—
　　Though a loyal one and brave,
And his laurels ne'er so fragrant
　　As when scattered o'er the grave.

LINES FOR AN ALBUM

I WOULD not trace the hackneyed phrase
Of shallow words and empty praise,
And prate of "peace" till one might think
My foolish pen was drunk with ink.
Nor will I here the wish express
Of "lasting love and happiness,"
And "cloudless skies"—for after all
"Into each life some rain must fall."
—No. Keep the empty page below,
In my remembrance, white as snow—
Nor sigh to know the secret prayer
My spirit hand has written there.

TO ANNIE

WHEN the lids of dusk are falling
    O'er the dreamy eyes of day,
And the whippoorwills are calling,
    And the lesson laid away,—
May Mem'ry soft and tender
    As the prelude of the night,
Bend over you and render
    As tranquil a delight.

FAME

I

ONCE, in a dream, I saw a man
    With haggard face and tangled hair,
And eyes that nursed as wild a care
As gaunt Starvation ever can;
And in his hand he held a wand
    Whose magic touch gave life and thought
    Unto a form his fancy wrought
And robed with coloring so grand,
    It seemed the reflex of some child
    Of Heaven, fair and undefiled—
    A face of purity and love—
    To woo him into worlds above:
And as I gazed with dazzled eyes,
    A gleaming smile lit up his lips
    As his bright soul from its eclipse
Went flashing into Paradise.
Then tardy Fame came through the door
And found a picture—nothing more.

II

And once I saw a man, alone,
    In abject poverty, with hand
Uplifted o'er a block of stone
    That took a shape at his command
And smiled upon him, fair and good—
A perfect work of womanhood,

158

Save that the eyes might never weep,
Nor weary hands be crossed in sleep,
Nor hair that fell from crown to wrist,
Be brushed away, caressed and kissed.
And as in awe I gazed on her,
   I saw the sculptor's chisel fall—
      I saw him sink, without a moan,
      Sink lifeless at the feet of stone,
And lie there like a worshiper.
   Fame crossed the threshold of the hall,
   And found a statue—that was all.

III

And once I saw a man who drew
   A gloom about him like a cloak,
And wandered aimlessly. The few
   Who spoke of him at all, but spoke
Disparagingly of a mind
The Fates had faultily designed:
Too indolent for modern times—
   Too fanciful, and full of whims—
For, talking to himself in rhymes,
   And scrawling never-heard-of hymns,
The idle life to which he clung
Was worthless as the songs he sung!
I saw him, in my vision, filled
   With rapture o'er a spray of bloom
   The wind threw in his lonely room;
And of the sweet perfume it spilled
He drank to drunkenness, and flung

His long hair back, and laughed and sung
And clapped his hands as children do
At fairy tales they listen to,
While from his flying quill there dripped
Such music on his manuscript
That he who listens to the words
May close his eyes and dream the birds
Are twittering on every hand
A language he can understand.
He journeyed on through life, unknown,
Without one friend to call his own;
He tired. No kindly hand to press
The cooling touch of tenderness
Upon his burning brow, nor lift
To his parched lips God's freest gift—
No sympathetic sob or sigh
Of trembling lips—no sorrowing eye
Looked out through tears to see him die.
And Fame her greenest laurels brought
To crown a head that heeded not.

And this is Fame! A thing, indeed,
That only comes when least the need:
The wisest minds of every age
The book of life from page to page
Have searched in vain; each lesson conned
Will promise it the page beyond—
Until the last, when dusk of night
Falls over it, and reason's light
Is smothered by that unknown friend
Who signs his *nom de plume,* The End.

AN EMPTY NEST

I FIND an old deserted nest,
  Half-hidden in the underbrush:
A withered leaf, in phantom jest,
  Has nestled in it like a thrush
With weary, palpitating breast.

I muse as one in sad surprise
  Who seeks his childhood's home once more,
And finds it in a strange disguise
  Of vacant rooms and naked floor,
With sudden tear-drops in his eyes.

An empty nest! It used to bear
  A happy burden, when the breeze
Of summer rocked it, and a pair
  Of merry tattlers told the trees
What treasures they had hidden there.

But Fancy, flitting through the gleams
  Of youth's sunshiny atmosphere,
Has fallen in the past, and seems,
  Like this poor leaflet nestled here,—
A phantom guest of empty dreams.

MY FATHER'S HALLS

MY father's halls, so rich and rare,
Are desolate and bleak and bare;
My father's heart and halls are one,
Since I, their life and light, am gone.

O, valiant knight, with hand of steel
And heart of gold, hear my appeal:
Release me from the spoiler's charms,
And bear me to my father's arms.

THE HARP OF THE MINSTREL

THE harp of the minstrel has never a tone
    As sad as the song in his bosom to-night,
For the magical touch of his fingers alone
    Can not waken the echoes that breathe it aright;
But oh! as the smile of the moon may impart
    A sorrow to one in an alien clime,
Let the light of the melody fall on the heart,
    And cadence his grief into musical rhyme.

The faces have faded, the eyes have grown dim
    That once were his passionate love and his pride;
And alas! all the smiles that once blossomed for him
    Have fallen away as the flowers have died.
The hands that entwined him the laureate's wreath
    And crowned him with fame in the long, long ago,
Like the laurels are withered and folded beneath
    The grass and the stubble—the frost and the
      snow.

Then sigh, if thou wilt, as the whispering strings
    Strive ever in vain for the utterance clear,
And think of the sorrowful spirit that sings,
    And jewel the song with the gem of a tear.

For the harp of the minstrel has never a tone
  As sad as the song in his bosom to-night,
And the magical touch of his fingers alone
  Can not waken the echoes that breathe it aright.

HONEY DRIPPING FROM THE COMB

H OW slight a thing may set one's fancy
            drifting
Upon the dead sea of the Past!—A view—
Sometimes an odor—or a rooster lifting
      A far-off *"Ooh! ooh-ooh!"*

And suddenly we find ourselves astray
  In some wood's-pasture of the Long Ago—
Or idly dream again upon a day
      Of rest we used to know.

I bit an apple but a moment since—
  A wilted apple that the worm had spurned,—
Yet hidden in the taste were happy hints
      Of good old days returned.—

And so my heart, like some enraptured lute,
  Tinkles a tune so tender and complete,
God's blessing must be resting on the fruit—
      So bitter, yet so sweet!

JOHN WALSH

A STRANGE life—strangely passed!
    We may not read the soul
When God has folded up the scroll
    In death at last.
We may not—dare not say of one
Whose task of life as well was done
As he could do it,—"This is lost,
And prayers may never pay the cost."

Who listens to the song
    That sings within the breast,
    Should ever hear the good expressed
        Above the wrong.
And he who leans an eager ear
To catch the discord, he will hear
The echoes of his own weak heart
Beat out the most discordant part.

Whose tender heart could build
    Affection's bower above
    A heart where baby nests of love
        Were ever filled,—

166

With upward growth may reach and twine
About the children, grown divine,
That once were his a time so brief
His very joy was more than grief.

O Sorrow—"Peace, be still!"
  God reads the riddle right;
  And we who grope in constant night
    But serve His will;
And when sometime the doubt is gone,
And darkness blossoms into dawn,—
"God keeps the good," we then will say:
" 'Tis but the dross He throws away."

ORLIE WILDE

A GODDESS, with a siren's grace,—
A sun-haired girl on a craggy place
Above a bay where fish-boats lay
Drifting about like birds of prey.

Wrought was she of a painter's dream,—
Wise only as are artists wise,
My artist-friend, Rolf Herschkelhiem,
With deep sad eyes of oversize,
And face of melancholy guise.

I pressed him that he tell to me
This masterpiece's history.
He turned—*re*turned—and thus beguiled
Me with the tale of Orlie Wilde:—

"We artists live ideally:
We breed our firmest facts of air;
We make our own reality—
We dream a thing and it is so.
The fairest scenes we ever see
Are mirages of memory;

The sweetest thoughts we ever know
We plagiarize from Long Ago:
And as the girl on canvas there
Is marvelously rare and fair,
'Tis only inasmuch as she
Is dumb and may not speak to me!"
He tapped me with his mahlstick—then
The picture,—and went on again:

"Orlie Wilde, the fisher's child—
I see her yet, as fair and mild
As ever nursling summer day
Dreamed on the bosom of the bay:
For I was twenty then, and went
Alone and long-haired—all content
With promises of sounding name
And fantasies of future fame,
And thoughts that now my mind discards
As editor a fledgling bard's.

"At evening once I chanced to go,
With pencil and portfolio,
Adown the street of silver sand
That winds beneath this craggy land,
To make a sketch of some old scurf
Of driftage, nosing through the surf
A splintered mast, with knarl and strand
Of rigging-rope and tattered threads
Of flag and streamer and of sail
That fluttered idly in the gale

Or whipped themselves to sadder shreds.
The while I wrought, half listlessly,
On my dismantled subject, came
A sea-bird, settling on the same
With plaintive moan, as though that he
Had lost his mate upon the sea;
And—with my melancholy trend—
It brought dim dreams half understood—
It wrought upon my morbid mood,—
I thought of my own voyagings
That had no end—that have no end.—
And, like the sea-bird, I made moan
That I was loveless and alone.
And when at last with weary wings
It went upon its wanderings,
With upturned face I watched its flight
Until this picture met my sight:
A goddess, with a siren's grace,—
A sun-haired girl on a craggy place
Above a bay where fish-boats lay
Drifting about like birds of prey.

"In airy poise she, gazing, stood
A matchless form of womanhood,
That brought a thought that if for me
Such eyes had sought across the sea,
I could have swum the widest tide
That ever mariner defied,
And, at the shore, could on have gone
To that high crag she stood upon,

To there entreat and say, 'My Sweet,
Behold thy servant at thy feet.'
And to my soul I said: 'Above,
There stands the idol of thy love!'

"In this rapt, awed, ecstatic state
I gazed—till lo! I was aware
A fisherman had joined her there—
A weary man, with halting gait,
Who toiled beneath a basket's weight:
Her father, as I guessed, for she
Had run to meet him gleefully
And ta'en his burden to herself,
That perched upon her shoulder's shelf
So lightly that she, tripping, neared
A jutting crag and disappeared;
But she left the echo of a song
That thrills me yet, and will as long
As I have being! . . .

. . . "Evenings came
And went,—but each the same—the same:
She watched above, and even so
I stood there watching from below;
· Till, grown so bold at last, I sung,—
(What matter now the theme thereof!)—
It brought an answer from her tongue—
Faint as the murmur of a dove,
Yet all the more the song of love. . . .

"I turned and looked upon the bay,
With palm to forehead—eyes a-blur
In the sea's smile—meant but for her!—
I saw the fish-boats far away
In misty distance, lightly drawn
In chalk-dots on the horizon—
Looked back at her, long, wistfully,—
And, pushing off an empty skiff,
I beckoned her to quit the cliff
And yield me her rare company
Upon a little pleasure-cruise.—
She stood, as loathful to refuse,
To muse for full a moment's time,—
Then answered back in pantomime
'She feared some danger from the sea
Were she discovered thus with me.'
I motioned then to ask her if
I might not join her on the cliff;
And back again, with graceful wave
Of lifted arm, she answer gave
'She feared some danger from the sea.'

"Impatient, piqued, impetuous, I
Sprang in the boat, and flung 'Good-by'
From pouted mouth with angry hand,
And madly pulled away from land
With lusty stroke, despite that she
Held out her hands entreatingly:
And when far out, with covert eye

I shoreward glanced, I saw her fly
In reckless haste adown the crag,
Her hair a-flutter like a flag
Of gold that danced across the strand
In little mists of silver sand.
All curious I, pausing, tried
To fancy what it all implied,—
When suddenly I found my feet
Were wet; and, underneath the seat
On which I sat, I heard the sound
Of gurgling waters, and I found
The boat aleak alarmingly. . . .
I turned and looked upon the sea,
Whose every wave seemed mocking me;
I saw the fishers' sails once more—
In dimmer distance than before;
I saw the sea-bird wheeling by,
With foolish wish that *I* could fly:
I thought of firm earth, home and friends—
I thought of everything that tends
To drive a man to frenzy and
To wholly lose his own command;
I thought of all my waywardness—
Thought of a mother's deep distress;
Of youthful follies yet unpurged—
Sins, as the seas, about me surged—
Thought of the printer's ready pen
To-morrow drowning me again;—
A million things without a name—
I thought of everything but—Fame. . . .

"A memory yet is in my mind,
So keenly clear and sharp-defined,
I picture every phase and line
Of life and death, and neither mine,—
While some fair seraph, golden-haired,
Bends over me,—with white arms bared,
That strongly plait themselves about
My drowning weight and lift me out—
With joy too great for words to state
Or tongue to dare articulate!

"And this seraphic ocean-child
And heroine was Orlie Wilde:
And thus it was I came to hear
Her voice's music in my ear—
Ay, thus it was Fate paved the way
That I walk desolate to-day!" . . .

The artist paused and bowed his face
Within his palms a little space,
While reverently on his form
I bent my gaze and marked a storm
That shook his frame as wrathfully
As some typhoon of agony,
And fraught with sobs—the more profound
For that peculiar laughing sound
We hear when strong men weep. . . . I leant
With warmest sympathy—I bent
To stroke with soothing hand his brow,
He murmuring—" 'Tis over now!—

And shall I tie the silken thread
Of my frail romance?" . "Yes," I said.—
He faintly smiled; and then, with brow
In kneading palm, as one in dread—
His tasseled cap pushed from his head;—
" 'Her voice's music,' I repeat,"
He said,—" 'twas sweet—O passing sweet!—
Though she herself, in uttering
Its melody, proved not the thing
Of loveliness my dreams made meet
For me—there, yearning, at her feet—
Prone at her feet—a worshiper,—
For lo! she spake a tongue," moaned he,
"Unknown to me;—unknown to me
As mine to her—as mine to her."

THAT OTHER MAUD MULLER

MAUD MULLER worked at making hay,
And cleared her forty cents a day.

Her clothes were coarse, but her health was fine,
And so she worked in the sweet sunshine

Singing as glad as a bird in May
"Barbara Allen" the livelong day.

She often glanced at the far-off town,
And wondered if eggs were up or down.

And the sweet song died of a strange disease,
Leaving a phantom taste of cheese,

And an appetite and a nameless ache
For soda-water and ginger cake.

The Judge rode slowly into view—
Stopped his horse in the shade and threw

His fine-cut out, while the blushing Maud
Marveled much at the kind he "chawed."

"He was dry as a fish," he said with a wink,
"And kind o' thought that a good square drink

Would brace him up." So the cup was filled
With the crystal wine that old spring spilled;

And she gave it him with a sun-browned hand.
"Thanks," said the Judge in accents bland;

"A thousand thanks! for a sweeter draught,
From a fairer hand"—but there he laughed.

And the sweet girl stood in the sun that day,
And raked the Judge instead of the hay.

A MAN OF MANY PARTS

IT was a man of many parts,
  Who in his coffer mind
Had stored the Classics and the Arts
  And Sciences combined;
The purest gems of poesy
  Came flashing from his pen—
The wholesome truths of History
  He gave his fellow men.

He knew the stars from "Dog" to Mars;
  And he could tell you, too,
Their distances—as though the cars
  Had often checked him through—
And time 'twould take to reach the sun,
  Or by the "Milky Way,"
Drop in upon the moon, or run
  The homeward trip, or stay.

With Logic at his fingers' ends,
  Theology in mind,
He often entertained his friends
  Until they died resigned;
And with inquiring mind intent
  Upon Alchemic arts
A dynamite experiment—

. . . .

A man of many parts!

THE FROG

WHO am I but the Frog—the Frog!
　　My realm is the dark bayou,
And my throne is the muddy and moss-grown log
　　That the poison-vine clings to—
And the blacksnakes slide in the slimy tide
　　Where the ghost of the moon looks blue.

What am I but a King—a King!—
　　For the royal robes I wear—
A scepter, too, and a signet-ring,
　　As vassals and serfs declare:
And a voice, god wot, that is equaled not
　　In the wide world anywhere!

I can talk to the Night—the Night!—
　　Under her big black wing
She tells me the tale of the world outright,
　　And the secret of everything;
For she knows you all, from the time you crawl
　　To the doom that death will bring.

The Storm swoops down, and he blows—and
    blows,—
  While I drum on his swollen cheek,
And croak in his angered eye that glows
  With the lurid lightning's streak;
While the rushes drown in the watery frown
  That his bursting passions leak.

And I can see through the sky—the sky—
  As clear as a piece of glass;
And I can tell you the how and why
  Of the things that come to pass—
And whether the dead are there instead,
  Or under the graveyard grass

To your Sovereign lord all hail—all hail!—
  To your Prince on his throne so grim!
Let the moon swing low, and the high stars trail
  Their heads in the dust to him;
And the wide world sing: Long live the King,
  And grace to his royal whim!

DEAD SELVES

HOW many of my selves are dead?
   The ghosts of many haunt me: Lo,
The baby in the tiny bed
With rockers on, is blanketed
   And sleeping in the long ago;
And so I ask, with shaking head,
How many of my selves are dead?

A little face with drowsy eyes
   And lisping lips comes mistily
From out the faded past, and tries
The prayers a mother breathed with sighs
   Of anxious care in teaching me;
But face and form and prayers have fled—
How many of my selves are dead?

The little naked feet that slipped
   In truant paths, and led the way
Through dead'ning pasture-lands, and tripped
O'er tangled poison-vines, and dipped
   In streams forbidden—where are they?
In vain I listen for their tread—
How many of my selves are dead?

The awkward boy the teacher caught
  Inditing letters filled with love,
Who was compelled, for all he fought,
To read aloud each tender thought
  Of "Sugar Lump" and "Turtle Dove."
I wonder where he hides his head—
How many of my selves are dead?

The earnest features of a youth
  With manly fringe on lip and chin,
With eager tongue to tell the truth,
To offer love and life, forsooth,
  So brave was he to woo and win;
A prouder man was never wed—
How many of my selves are dead?

The great, strong hands so all-inclined
  To welcome toil, or smooth the care
From mother-brows, or quick to find
A leisure-scrap of any kind,
  To toss the baby in the air,
Or clap at babbling things it said—
How many of my selves are dead?

The pact of brawn and scheming brain—
  Conspiring in the plots of wealth,
Still delving, till the lengthened chain,
Unwindlassed in the mines of gain,
  Recoils with dregs of ruined health
And pain and poverty instead—
How many of my selves are dead?

A—13

The faltering step, the faded hair—
   Head, heart and soul, all echoing
With maundering fancies that declare
That life and love were never there,
   Nor ever joy in anything,
Nor wounded heart that ever bled—
How many of my selves are dead?

So many of my selves are dead,
   That, bending here above the brink
Of my last grave, with dizzy head,
I find my spirit comforted,
   For all the idle things I think:
It can but be a peaceful bed,
Since all my other selves are dead.

A DREAM OF LONG AGO

LYING listless in the mosses
    Underneath a tree that tosses
Flakes of sunshine, and embosses
    Its green shadow with the snow—
Drowsy-eyed, I sink in slumber
Born of fancies without number—
Tangled fancies that encumber
    Me with dreams of long ago.

Ripples of the river singing;
And the water-lilies swinging
Bells of Parian, and ringing
    Peals of perfume faint and fine,
While old forms and fairy faces
Leap from out their hiding-places
In the past, with glad embraces
    Fraught with kisses sweet as wine.

Willows dip their slender fingers
O'er the little fisher's stringers,
While he baits his hook and lingers
    Till the shadows gather dim;
And afar off comes a calling

Like the sounds of water falling,
With the lazy echoes drawling
  Messages of haste to him.

Littie naked feet that tinkle
Through the stubble-fields, and twinkle
Down the winding road, and sprinkle
  Little mists of dusty rain,
While in pasture-lands the cattle
Cease their grazing with a rattle
Of the bells whose clappers tattle
  To their masters down the lane.

Trees that hold their tempting treasures
O'er the orchard's hedge embrasures,
Furnish their forbidden pleasures
  As in Eden lands of old;
And the coming of the master
Indicates a like disaster
To the frightened heart that faster
  Beats pulsations manifold.

Puckered lips whose pipings tingle
In staccato notes that mingle
Musically with the jingle-
  Haunted winds that lightly fan
Mellow twilights, crimson-tinted
By the sun, and picture-printed
Like a book that sweetly hinted
  Of the Nights Arabian.

Porticoes with columns plaited
And entwined with vines and freighted
With a bloom all radiated
  With the light of moon and star;
Where some tender voice is winging
In sad flights of song, and singing
To the dancing fingers flinging
  Dripping from the sweet guitar.

Would my dreams were never taken
From me: that with faith unshaken
I might sleep and never waken
  On a weary world of woe!
Links of love would never sever
As I dreamed them, never, never!
I would glide along forever
  Through the dreams of long ago.

CRAQUEODOOM

THE Crankadox leaned o'er the edge of the
      moon
  And wistfully gazed on the sea
Where the Gryxabodill madly whistled a tune
  To the air of "Ti-fol-de-ding-dee."
The quavering shriek of the Fly-up-the-creek
  Was fitfully wafted afar
To the Queen of the Wunks as she powdered her
     cheek
  With the pulverized rays of a star.

The Gool closed his ear on the voice of the Grig,
  And his heart it grew heavy as lead
As he marked the Baldekin adjusting his wing
  On the opposite side of his head,
And the air it grew chill as the Gryxabodill
  Raised his dank, dripping fins to the skies,
And plead with the Plunk for the use of her bill
  To pick the tears out of his eyes.

The ghost of the Zhack flitted by in a trance,
  And the Squidjum hid under a tub

As he heard the loud hooves of the Hooken ad-
     vance
  With a rub-a-dub—dub-a-dub—dub!
And the Crankadox cried, as he lay down and died,
  "My fate there is none to bewail,"
While the Queen of the Wunks drifted over the
     tide
  With a long piece of crape to her tail.

JUNE

O QUEENLY month of indolent repose!
    I drink thy breath in sips of rare perfume,
  As in thy downy lap of clover-bloom
I nestle like a drowsy child and doze
The lazy hours away. The zephyr throws
  The shifting shuttle of the Summer's loom
  And weaves a damask-work of gleam and gloom
Before thy listless feet. The lily blows
A bugle-call of fragrance o'er the glade;
  And, wheeling into ranks, with plume and spear,
Thy harvest-armies gather on parade;
  While, faint and far away, yet pure and clear,
A voice calls out of alien lands of shade:—
  All hail the Peerless Goddess of the Year!

WASH LOWRY'S REMINISCENCE

AND you're the poet of this concern?
　　I've seed your name in print
A dozen times, but I'll be dern
　　I'd 'a' never 'a' took the hint
O' the size you are—fer I'd pictured you
　　A kind of a tallish man—
Dark-complected and sallor too,
　　And on the consumpted plan.

'Stid o' that you're little and small,
　　With a milk-and-water face—
'Thout no snap in your eyes at all,
　　Er nothin' to suit the case!
Kind o' look like a—I don't know—
　　One o' these fair-ground chaps
That runs a thingamajig to blow,
　　Er a candy-stand perhaps.

191

'Ll I've allus thought that poetry
    Was a sort of a—some disease—
Fer I knowed a poet once, and he
    Was techy and hard to please,
And moody-like, and kind o' sad
    And didn't seem to mix
With other folks—like his health was bad,
    Er his liver out o' fix.

Used to teach fer a livelihood—
    There's folks in Pipe Crick yit
Remembers him—and he was good
    At cipherin' I'll admit—
And posted up in G'ography
    But when it comes to tact,
And gittin' along with the school, you see,
    He fizzled, and that's a fact!

Boarded with us fer fourteen months
    And in all that time I'll say
We never catched him a-sleepin' once
    Er idle a single day.
But shucks! It made him worse and worse
    A-writin' rhymes and stuff,
And the school committee used to furse
    'At the school warn't good enough.

He warn't as strict as he ought to been,
    And never was known to whip,
Or even to keep a scholard in
    At work at his penmanship;

'Stid o' that he'd learn 'em notes,
　　And have 'em every day,
Spilin' hymns and a-splittin' th'oats
　　With his "Do-sol-fa-me-ra!"

Tel finally it was jest agreed
　　We'd have to let him go,
And we all felt bad—we did indeed,
　　When we come to tell him so;
Fer I remember, he turned so white,
　　And smiled so sad, somehow,
I someway felt it wasn't right,
　　And I'm shore it wasn't now!

He hadn't no complaints at all—
　　He bid the school adieu,
And all o' the scholards great and small
　　Was mighty sorry too!
And when he closed that afternoon
　　They sung some lines that he
Had writ a purpose, to some old tune
　　That suited the case, you see.

And then he lingered and delayed
　　And wouldn't go away—
And shet himself in his room and stayed
　　A-writin' from day to day;
And kep' a gittin' stranger still,
　　And thinner all the time,
You know, as any feller will
　　On nothin' else but rhyme.

He didn't seem adzactly right,
  Er like he was crossed in love,
He'd work away night after night,
  And walk the floor above;
We'd hear him read and talk, and sing
  So lonesome-like and low,
My woman's cried like ever'thing—
  'Way in the night, you know.

And when at last he tuck to bed
  He'd have his ink and pen;
"So's he could coat the muse" he said,
  "He'd die contented then";
And jest before he past away
  He read with dyin' gaze
The epitaph that stands to-day
  To show you where he lays.

And ever sence then I've allus thought
  That poetry's some disease,
And them like you that's got it ought
  To watch their q's and p's;
And leave the sweets of rhyme, to sup
  On the wholesome draughts of toil,
And git your health recruited up
  By plowin' in rougher soil.

THE ANCIENT PRINTERMAN

"O PRINTERMAN of sallow face,
　　And look of absent guile,
Is it the 'copy' on your 'case'
　　That causes you to smile?
Or is it some old treasure scrap
　　You cull from Memory's file?

"I fain would guess its mystery—
　　For often I can trace
A fellow dreamer's history
　　Whene'er it haunts the face;
Your fancy's running riot
　　In a retrospective race!

"Ah, Printerman, you're straying
　　Afar from 'stick' and type—
Your heart has 'gone a-maying,'
　　And you taste old kisses, ripe
Again on lips that pucker
　　At your old asthmatic pipe!

"You are dreaming of old pleasures
   That have faded from your view;
And the music-burdened measures
   Of the laughs you listen to
Are now but angel-echoes—
   O, have I spoken true?"

The ancient Printer hinted
   With a motion full of grace
To where the words were printed
   On a card above his "case,"—
"I am deaf and dumb!" I left him
   With a smile upon his face.

PRIOR TO MISS BELLE'S APPEARANCE

WHAT makes you come *here* fer, Mister,
    So much to *our* house?—*Say?*
Come to see our big sister!—
An' Charley he says 'at you kissed her
    An' he ketched you, th'uther day!—
Didn' you, Charley?—But we p'omised Belle
An' crossed our heart to never to tell—
'Cause *she* gived us some o' them-er
Chawk'lut-drops 'at you bringed to her!

Charley he's my little b'uther—
    An' we has a-mostest fun,
Don't we, Charley?—Our Muther,
Whenever we whips one anuther,
    Tries to whip *us*—an' we *run*—
Don't we, Charley?—An' nen, bime-by,
Nen she gives us cake—an' pie—
Don't she, Charley?—when we come in
An' p'omise never to do it ag'in!

He's named Charley.—I'm *Willie*—
  An' I'm got the purtiest name!
But Uncle Bob *he* calls me "Billy"—
Don't he, Charley?—'N' our filly
  We named "Billy," the same
Ist like me! An' our Ma said
'At "Bob puts foolishnuss into our head!"—
Didn' she, Charley?—An' *she* don't know
Much about *boys!*—'Cause Bob said so!

Baby's a funniest feller!
  Nain't no hair on his head—
Is they, Charley?—It's meller
Wite up there! An' ef Belle er
  Us ask wuz *we* that way, Ma said,—
"Yes; an' yer *Pa's* head wuz soft as that,
An' it's that way yet!"—An' Pa grabs his hat
An' says, "Yes childern, she's right about Pa—
'Cause that's the reason he married yer Ma!"

An' our Ma says 'at "Belle couldn'
  Ketch nothin' at all but ist *'bows'!"*—
An' *Pa* says 'at "you're soft as puddun!"—
An' *Uncle Bob* says "you're a good-un—
  'Cause he can tell by yer nose!"—
Didn' he, Charley?—An' when Belle'll play
In the poller on th' pianer, some day,
Bob makes up funny songs about you,
Till she gits mad—like he wants her to!

Our sister *Fanny* she's *'leven*
   Years old! 'At's mucher 'an *I*—
Ain't it, Charley? . . . I'm seven!—
But our sister Fanny's in *Heaven!*
   Nere's where you go ef you die!—
Don't you, Charley?—Nen you has *wings*—
Ist like Fanny!—an' *purtiest things!*—
Don't you, Charley?—An' nen you can *fly*—
Ist fly—an' *ever*'thing! . . . Wisht *I'd* die!

WHEN MOTHER COMBED MY HAIR

WHEN Memory, with gentle hand,
    Has led me to that foreign land
Of childhood days, I long to be
Again the boy on bended knee,
With head a-bow, and drowsy smile
Hid in a mother's lap the while,
With tender touch and kindly care,
She bends above and combs my hair.

Ere threats of Time, or ghosts of cares
Had paled it to the hue it wears,
Its tangled threads of amber light
Fell o'er a forehead, fair and white,
That only knew the light caress
Of loving hands, or sudden press
Of kisses that were sifted there
The times when mother combed my hair.

But its last gleams of gold have slipped
Away; and Sorrow's manuscript
Is fashioned of the snowy brow—
So lined and underscored now

That you, to see it, scarce would guess
It e'er had felt the fond caress
Of loving lips, or known the care
Of those dear hands that combed my hair.

.　　.　　.　　.　　.　　.　　.　　.

I am so tired! Let me be
A moment at my mother's knee;
One moment—that I may forget
The trials waiting for me yet:
One moment free from every pain—
O! Mother! Comb my hair again!
And I will, oh, so humbly bow,
For I've a wife that combs it now.

A WRANGDILLION

DEXERY-TETHERY! down in the dike,
   Under the ooze and the slime,
Nestles the wraith of a reticent Gryke,
   Blubbering bubbles of rhyme:
Though the reeds touch him and tickle his teeth—
   Though the Graigroll and the Cheest
Pluck at the leaves of his laureate-wreath,
   Nothing affects him the least.

He sinks to the dregs in the dead o' the night,
   And he shuffles the shadows about
As he gathers the stars in a nest of delight
   And sets there and hatches them out:
The Zhederrill peers from his watery mine
   In scorn with the Will-o'-the-wisp,
As he twinkles his eyes in a whisper of shine
   That ends in a luminous lisp.

The Morning is born like a baby of gold,
  And it lies in a spasm of pink,
And rallies the Cheest for the horrible cold
  He has dragged to the willowy brink,
The Gryke blots his tears with a scrap of his
    grief,
  And growls at the wary Graigroll
As he twunkers a tune on a Tiljicum leaf
  And hums like a telegraph pole.

GEORGE MULLEN'S CONFESSION

FOR the sake of guilty conscience, and the heart
    that ticks the time
Of the clockworks of my nature, I desire to say
    that I'm
A weak and sinful creature, as regards my daily
    walk
The last five years and better. It ain't worth while
    to talk—

I've been too mean to tell it! I've been so hard,
    you see,
And full of pride, and—onry—now there's the word
    for me—
Just onry—and to show you, I'll give my history
With vital points in question, and I think you'll all
    agree.

I was always stiff and stubborn since I could recol-
    lect,
And had an awful temper, and never would reflect;
And always into trouble—I remember once at
    school
The teacher tried to flog me, and I reversed that
    rule.

O I was bad I tell you! And it's a funny move
That a fellow wild as I was could ever fall in love;
And it's a funny notion that an animal like me,
Under a girl's weak fingers was as tame as tame
    could be!

But it's so, and sets me thinking of the easy way
    she had
Of cooling down my temper—though I'd be fight-
    ing mad.
"My Lion Queen" I called her—when a spell of
    mine occurred
She'd come in a den of feelings and quell them
    with a word.

I'll tell you how she loved me—and what her peo-
    ple thought:
When I asked to marry Annie they said "they reck-
    oned not—
That I cut too many didoes and monkey-shines to
    suit
Their idea of a son-in-law, and I could go, to boot!"

I tell you that thing riled me! Why, I felt my face
    turn white,
And my teeth shut like a steel trap, and the fingers
    of my right
Hand pained me with their pressure—all the rest's
    a mystery
Till I heard my Annie saying—"I'm going, too, you
    see."

We were coming through the gateway, and she
    wavered for a spell
When she heard her mother crying and her raving
    father yell
That she wa'n't no child of his'n—like an actor in
    a play
We saw at Independence, coming through the other
    day.

Well! that's the way we started. And for days
    and weeks and months
And even years we journeyed on, regretting never
    once
Of starting out together upon the path of life—
A kind o' sort o' husband, but a mighty loving
    wife,—

And the cutest little baby—little Grace—I see her
    now
A-standin' on the pig-pen as her mother milked the
    cow—
And I can hear her shouting—as I stood unloading
    straw,—
"I'm ain't as big as papa, but I'm biggerest'n ma."

Now folks that never married don't seem to under-
    stand
That a little baby's language is the sweetest ever
    planned—

Why, I tell you it's pure music, and I'll just go on
    to say
That I sometimes have a notion that the angels talk
    that way!

There's a chapter in this story I'd be happy to de-
    stroy;
I could burn it up before you with a mighty sight
    of joy;
But I'll go ahead and give it—not in detail, no, my
    friend,
For it takes five years of reading before you find
    the end.

My Annie's folks relented—at least, in some de-
    gree;
They sent one time for Annie, but they didn't send
    for me.
The old man wrote the message with a heart as hot
    and dry
As a furnace—"Annie Mullen, come and see your
    mother die."

I saw the slur intended—why I fancied I could see
The old man shoot the insult like a poison dart at
    me;
And in that heat of passion I swore an inward oath
That if Annie pleased her father she could never
    please us both.

I watched her—dark and sullen—as she hurried on
    her shawl;
I watched her—calm and cruel, though I saw her
    tear-drops fall;
I watched her—cold and heartless, though I heard
    her moaning, call
For mercy from high Heaven—and I smiled
    throughout it all.

Why even when she kissed me, and her tears were
    on my brow,
As she murmured, "George, forgive me—I must go
    to mother now!"
Such hate there was within me that I answered not
    at all,
But calm, and cold and cruel, I smiled throughout
    it all.

But a shadow in the doorway caught my eye, and
    then the face
Full of innocence and sunshine of little baby Grace.
And I snatched her up and kissed her, and I soft-
    ened through and through
For a minute when she told me "I must kiss her
    muvver too."

I remember, at the starting, how I tried to freeze
    again
As I watched them slowly driving down the little,
    crooked lane—

When Annie shouted something that ended in a
    cry,
And how I tried to whistle and it fizzled in a sigh.

I remember running after, with a glimmer in my
    sight—
Pretending I'd discovered that the traces wasn't
    right;
And the last that I remember, as they disappeared
    from view,
Was little Grace a-calling, "I see papa! Howdy-
    do!"

And left alone to ponder, I again took up my hate
For the old man who would chuckle that I was
    desolate;
And I mouthed my wrongs in mutters till my pride
    called up the pain
His last insult had given me—until I smiled again

Till the wild beast in my nature was raging in the
    den—
With no one now to quell it, and I wrote a letter
    then
Full of hissing things, and heated with so hot a heat
    of hate
That my pen flashed out black lightning at a most
    terrific rate.

I wrote that "she had wronged me when she went
 away from me—
Though to see her dying mother 'twas her father's
 victory,
And a woman that could waver when her husband's
 pride was rent
Was no longer worthy of it." And I shut the house
 and went.

To tell of my long exile would be of little good—
Though I couldn't half-way tell it, and I wouldn't
 if I could!
I could tell of California—of a wild and vicious
 life;
Of trackless plains, and mountains, and the Indian's scalping-knife.

I could tell of gloomy forests howling wild with
 threats of death;
I could tell of fiery deserts that have scorched me
 with their breath;
I could tell of wretched outcasts by the hundreds,
 great and small,
And could claim the nasty honor of the greatest of
 them all.

I could tell of toil and hardship; and of sickness
 and disease,
And hollow-eyed starvation, but I tell you, friend,
 that these

Are trifles in comparison with what a fellow feels
With that bloodhound, Remorsefulness, forever at
    his heels.

I remember—worn and weary of the long, long
    years of care,
When the frost of time was making early harvest of
    my hair—
I remember, wrecked and hopeless of a rest be-
    neath the sky,
My resolve to quit the country, and to seek the
    East, and die.

I remember my long journey, like a dull, oppres-
    sive dream,
Across the empty prairies till I caught the distant
    gleam
Of a city in the beauty of its broad and shining
    stream
On whose bosom, flocked together, float the mighty
    swans of steam.

I remember drifting with them till I found myself
    again
In the rush and roar and rattle of the engine and
    the train;
And when from my surroundings something spoke
    of child and wife,
It seemed the train was rumbling through a tunnel
    in my life.

Then I remember something—like a sudden burst
    of light—
That don't exactly tell it, but I couldn't tell it
    right—
A something clinging to me with its arms around
    my neck—
A little girl, for instance—or an angel, I expect—

For she kissed me, cried and called me "her dear
    papa," and I felt
My heart was pure virgin gold, and just about to
    melt—
And so it did—it melted in a mist of gleaming rain
When she took my hand and whispered, "My
    mama's on the train."

There's some things I can dwell on, and get off
    pretty well,
But the balance of this story I know I couldn't tell;
So I ain't going to try it, for to tell the reason
    why—
I'm so chicken-hearted lately I'd be certain 'most.
    to cry.

"TIRED OUT"

"TIRED out!" Yet face and brow
  Do not look aweary now,
And the eyelids lie like two
Pure, white rose-leaves washed with dew.
Was her life so hard a task?—
Strange that we forget to ask
What the lips now dumb for aye
Could have told us yesterday!

"Tired out!" A faded scrawl
Pinned upon the ragged shawl—
Nothing else to leave a clue
Even of a friend or two,
Who might come to fold the hands,
Or smooth back the dripping strands
Of her tresses, or to wet
Them anew with fond regret.

"Tired out!" We can but guess
Of her little happiness—
Long ago, in some fair land,
When a lover held her hand
In the dream that frees us all,
Soon or later, from its thrall—
Be it either false or true,
We, at last, must tire, too.

HARLIE

FOLD the little waxen hands
  Lightly. Let your warmest tears
Speak regrets, but never fears,—
  Heaven understands!
Let the sad heart, o'er the tomb,
Lift again and burst in bloom
Fragrant with a prayer as sweet
As the lily at your feet.

Bend and kiss the folded eyes—
They are only feigning sleep
While their truant glances peep
  Into Paradise.
See, the face, though cold and white,
Holds a hint of some delight
E'en with Death, whose finger-tips
Rest upon the frozen lips.

When, within the years to come,
Vanished echoes live once more—
Pattering footsteps on the floor,
  And the sounds of home,—
Let your arms in fancy fold
Little Harlie as of old—
As of old and as he waits
At the City's golden gates.

SAY SOMETHING TO ME

SAY something to me! I've waited so
    long—
  Waited and wondered in vain;
Only a sentence would fall like a song
  Over this listening pain—
Over a silence that glowers and frowns,—
  Even my pencil to-night
Slips in the dews of my sorrow and wounds
  Each tender word that I write.

Say something to me—if only to tell
  Me you remember the past;
Let the sweet words, like the notes of a bell,
  Ring out my vigil at last.
O it were better, far better than this
  Doubt and distrust in the breast,—
For in the wine of a fanciful kiss
  I could taste Heaven, and—rest.

Say something to me! I kneel and I plead,
  In my wild need, for a word;
If my poor heart from this silence were
    freed,
  I could soar up like a bird
In the glad morning, and twitter and sing,
  Carol and warble and cry
Blithe as the lark as he cruises awing
  Over the deeps of the sky.

LEONAINIE

LEONAINIE—Angels named her;
   And they took the light
Of the laughing stars and framed her
  In a smile of white;
    And they made her hair of gloomy
    Midnight, and her eyes of bloomy
    Moonshine, and they brought her to
      me
  In the solemn night.—

In a solemn night of summer,
  When my heart of gloom
Blossomed up to greet the comer
  Like a rose in bloom;
    All forebodings that distressed me
    I forgot as Joy caressed me—
    (*Lying* Joy! that caught and pressed
      me
  In the arms of doom!)

Only spake the little lisper
  In the Angel-tongue;
Yet I, listening, heard her whisper,—
  "Songs are only sung

Here below that they may grieve
    you—
Tales but told you to deceive you,—
So must Leonainie leave you
While her love is young."

Then God smiled and it was morning.
    Matchless and supreme
Heaven's glory seemed adorning
    Earth with its esteem:
        Every heart but mine seemed gifted
        With the voice of prayer, and lifted
        Where my Leonainie drifted
    From me like a dream.

A TEST OF LOVE

"Now who shall say he loves me not."

H E wooed her first in an atmosphere
    Of tender and low-breathed sighs;
But the pang of her laugh went cutting clear
    To the soul of the enterprise;
"You beg so pert for the kiss you seek
    It reminds me, John," she said,
"Of a poodle pet that jumps to 'speak'
    For a crumb or a crust of bread."

And flashing up, with the blush that flushed
    His face like a tableau-light,
Came a bitter threat that his white lips
        hushed
    To a chill, hoarse-voiced "Good night!"
And again her laugh, like a knell that tolled,
    And a wide-eyed mock surprise,—
"Why, John," she said, "you have taken
        cold
    In the chill air of your sighs!"

And then he turned, and with teeth tight-
    clenched,
  He told her he hated her,—
That his love for her from his heart he
    wrenched
  Like a corpse from a sepulcher.
And then she called him "a ghoul all red
  With the quintessence of crimes"—
"But I know you love me now," she said,
  And kissed him a hundred times.

FATHER WILLIAM

A NEW VERSION BY LEE O. HARRIS AND JAMES
WHITCOMB RILEY

"YOU are old, Father William, and though one
would think
All the veins in your body were dry,
Yet the end of your nose is red as a pink;
I beg your indulgence, but why?"

"You see," Father William replied, "in my youth—
'Tis a thing I must ever regret—
It worried me so to keep up with the truth
That my nose has a flush on it yet."

"You are old," said the youth, "and I grieve to de-
tect
A feverish gleam in your eye;
Yet I'm willing to give you full time to reflect.
Now, pray, can you answer me why?"

"Alas," said the sage, "I was tempted to choose
Me a wife in my earlier years,
And the grief, when I think that she didn't refuse,
Has reddened my eyelids with tears."

220

"You are old, Father William," the young man said,
    "And you never touch wine, you declare,
Yet you sleep with your feet at the head of the bed;
    Now answer me that if you dare."

"In my youth," said the sage, "I was told it was
        true,
    That the world turned around in the night;
I cherished the lesson, my boy, and I knew
    That at morning my feet would be right."

"You are old," said the youth, "and it grieved me to
        note,
    As you recently fell through the door,
That 'full as a goose' had been chalked on your
        coat;
    Now answer me that I implore."

"My boy," said the sage, "I have answered you fair,
    While you stuck to the point in dispute,
But this is a personal matter, and there
    Is my answer—the toe of my boot."

WHAT THE WIND SAID

I *MUSE to-day, in a listless way,*
  In the gleam of a summer land;
I close my eyes as a lover may
  At the touch of his sweetheart's hand,
And I hear these things in the whisperings
  Of the zephyrs round me fanned:—

I am the Wind, and I rule mankind,
  And I hold a sovereign reign
Over the lands, as God designed,
  And the waters they contain:
Lo! the bound of the wide world round
  Falleth in my domain!

I was born on a stormy morn
  In a kingdom walled with snow,
Whose crystal cities laugh to scorn
  The proudest the world can show;
And the daylight's glare is frozen there
  In the breath of the blasts that blow.

222

Life to me was a jubilee
  From the first of my youthful days:
Clinking my icy toys with glee—
  Playing my childish plays;
Filling my hands with the silver sands
  To scatter a thousand ways:

Chasing the flakes that the Polar shakes
  From his shaggy coat of white,
Or hunting the trace of the track he makes
  And sweeping it from sight,
As he turned to glare from the slippery stair
  Of the iceberg's farthest height.

Till I grew so strong that I strayed ere long
  From my home of ice and chill;
With an eager heart and a merry song
  I traveled the snows until
I heard the thaws in the ice-crag's jaws
  Crunched with a hungry will;

And the angry crash of the waves that dash
  Themselves on the jaggèd shore
Where the splintered masts of the ice-wrecks
    flash,
  And the frightened breakers roar
In wild unrest on the ocean's breast
  For a thousand leagues or more.

And the grand old sea invited me
  With a million beckoning hands,
And I spread my wings for a flight as free
  As ever a sailor plans
When his thoughts are wild and his heart be-
    guiled
  With the dreams of foreign lands.

I passed a ship on its homeward trip,
  With a weary and toil-worn crew;
And I kissed their flag with a welcome lip,
  And so glad a gale I blew
That the sailors quaffed their grog and
    laughed
  At the work I made them do.

I drifted by where sea-groves lie
  Like brides in the fond caress
Of the warm sunshine and the tender sky—
  Where the ocean, passionless
And tranquil, lies like a child whose eyes
  Are blurred with drowsiness.

I drank the air and the perfume there,
  And bathed in a fountain's spray;
And I smoothed the wings and the plumage
    rare
  Of a bird for his roundelay,
And fluttered a rag from a signal-crag
  For a wretched castaway.

With a sea-gull resting on my breast,
  I launched on a madder flight:
And I lashed the waves to a wild unrest,
  And howled with a fierce delight
Till the daylight slept; and I wailed and
    wept
  Like a fretful babe all night.

For I heard the boom of a gun strike doom;
  And the gleam of a blood-red star
Glared at me through the mirk and gloom
  From the lighthouse tower afar;
And I held my breath at the shriek of death
  That came from the harbor bar.

For I am the Wind, and I rule mankind,
  And I hold a sovereign reign
Over the lands, as God designed,
  And the waters they contain:
Lo! the bound of the wide world round
  Falleth in my domain!

I journeyed on, when the night was gone,
  O'er a coast of oak and pine;
And I followed a path that a stream had
    drawn
  Through a land of vale and vine,
And here and there was a village fair
  In a nest of shade and shine.

I passed o'er lakes where the sunshine shakes
  And shivers his golden lance
On the glittering shield of the wave that
    breaks
Where the fish-boats dip and dance,
And the trader sails where the mist unveils
  The glory of old romance.

I joyed to stand where the jeweled hand
  Of the maiden-morning lies
On the tawny brow of the mountain-land.
  Where the eagle shrieks and cries,
And holds his throne to himself alone
  From the light of human eyes.

Adown deep glades where the forest shades
  Are dim as the dusk of day—
Where only the foot of the wild beast wades,
  Or the Indian dares to stray,
As the blacksnakes glide through the reeds
    and hide
  In the swamp-depths grim and gray.

And I turned and fled from the place of
    dread
  To the far-off haunts of men.
"In the city's heart is rest," I said,—
  But I found it not, and when
I saw but care and vice reign there
  I was filled with wrath again:

And I blew a spark in the midnight dark
 Till it flashed to an angry flame
And scarred the sky with a lurid mark
 As red as the blush of shame:
And a hint of hell was the dying yell
 That up from the ruins came.

The bells went wild, and the black smoke
      piled
 Its pillars against the night,
Till I gathered them, like flocks defiled,
 And scattered them left and right,
While the holocaust's red tresses tossed
 As a maddened Fury's might.

"Ye overthrown!" did I jeer and groan—
 "Ho! who is your master?—say!—
Ye shapes that writhe in the slag and moan
 Your slow-charred souls away—
Ye worse than worst of things accurst
 Ye dead leaves of a day!"

I am the Wind, and I rule mankind,
 And I hold a sovereign reign
Over the lands, as God designed,
 And the waters they contain:
Lo! the bound of the wide world round
 Falleth in my domain!

  .   .   .   .

I wake, as one from a dream half done,
And gaze with a dazzled eye
On an autumn leaf like a scrap of sun
That the wind goes whirling by,
While afar I hear, with a chill of fear,
The winter storm-king sigh,

MORTON

THE warm pulse of the nation has grown
    chill;
The muffled heart of Freedom, like a knell,
Throbs solemnly for one whose earthly will
    Wrought every mission well.

Whose glowing reason towered above the sea
    Of dark disaster like a beacon light,
And led the Ship of State, unscathed and free,
    Out of the gulfs of night.

When Treason, rabid-mouthed, and fanged with
    steel,
    Lay growling o'er the bones of fallen braves,
And when beneath the tyrant's iron heel
    Were ground the hearts of slaves,

And War, with all his train of horrors, leapt
    Across the fortress-walls of Liberty
With havoc e'en the marble goddess wept
    With tears of blood to see.

Throughout it all his brave and kingly mind
　Kept loyal vigil o'er the patriot's vow,
And yet the flag he lifted to the wind
　Is drooping o'er him now.

And Peace—all pallid from the battle-field
　When first again it hovered o'er the land
And found his voice above it like a shield,
　Had nestled in his hand.

. . . .

O throne of State and gilded Senate halls—
　Though thousands throng your aisles and gal-
　　leries—
How empty are ye! and what silence falls
　On your hilarities!

And yet, though great the loss to us appears,
　The consolation sweetens all our pain—
Though hushed the voice, through all the coming
　　years
　Its echoes will remain.

AN AUTUMNAL EXTRAVAGANZA

WITH a sweeter voice than birds
　　Dare to twitter in their sleep,
Pipe for me a tune of words,
　Till my dancing fancies leap
Into freedom vaster far
Than the realms of Reason are!
Sing for me with wilder fire
　Than the lover ever sung,
From the time he twanged the lyre
　When the world was baby-young.

O my maiden Autumn, you—
You have filled me through and through
With a passion so intense,
All of earthly eloquence
　Fails, and falls, and swoons away
In your presence. Like as one
Who essays to look the sun
　Fairly in the face, I say,
Though my eyes you dazzle blind
Greater dazzled is my mind.
So, my Autumn, let me kneel
　At your feet and worship you!
Be my sweetheart; let me feel
A—16

Your caress; and tell me too
Why your smiles bewilder me—
Glancing into laughter, then
Trancing into calm again,
Till your meaning drowning lies
In the dim depths of your eyes.
Let me see the things you see
Down the depths of mystery!
Blow aside the hazy veil
    From the daylight of your face
With the fragrance-ladened gale
    Of your spicy breath and chase
    Every dimple to its place.
Lift your gipsy finger-tips
To the roses of your lips,
And fling down to me a bud—
    But an unblown kiss—but one—
It shall blossom in my blood,
    Even after life is done—
When I dare to touch the brow
Your rare hair is veiling now—
When the rich, red-golden strands
Of the treasure in my hands
Shall be all of worldly worth
Heaven lifted from the earth,
Like a banner to have set
On its highest minaret.

THE ROSE

IT tossed its head at the wooing breeze;
   And the sun, like a bashful swain,
Beamed on it through the waving trees
   With a passion all in vain,—
For my rose laughed in a crimson glee,
And hid in the leaves in wait for me.

The honey-bee came there to sing
   His love through the languid hours,
And vaunt of his hives, as a proud old king
   Might boast of his palace-towers:
But my rose bowed in a mockery,
And hid in the leaves in wait for me.

The humming-bird, like a courtier gay,
   Dipped down with a dalliant song,
And twanged his wings through the roundelay
   Of love the whole day long:
Yet my rose turned from his minstrelsy
And hid in the leaves in wait for me.

The firefly came in the twilight dim
  My red, red rose to woo—
Till quenched was the flame of love in him,
  And the light of his lantern too,
As my rose wept with dewdrops three
And hid in the leaves in wait for me.

And I said: I will cull my own sweet rose—
  Some day I will claim as mine
The priceless worth of the flower that knows
  No change, but a bloom divine—
The bloom of a fadeless constancy
That hides in the leaves in wait for me!

But time passed by in a strange disguise,
  And I marked it not, but lay
In a lazy dream, with drowsy eyes,
  Till the summer slipped away,
And a chill wind sang in a minor key:
"Where is the rose that waits for thee?"

.   .   .   .

I dream to-day, o'er a purple stain
  Of bloom on a withered stalk,
Pelted down by the autumn rain
  In the dust of the garden-walk,
That an Angel-rose in the world to be
Will hide in the leaves in wait for me.

THE MERMAN

I

WHO would be
A merman gay,
Singing alone,
Sitting alone,
With a mermaid's knee,
For instance—hey—
For a throne?

II

I would be a merman gay;
I would sit and sing the whole day long;
I would fill my lungs with the strongest brine,
And squirt it up in a spray of song,
And soak my head in my liquid voice;
I'd curl my tail in curves divine,
And let each curve in a kink rejoice.
I'd tackle the mermaids under the sea,
And yank 'em around till they yanked me,
Sportively, sportively;
And then we would wiggle away, away,
To the pea-green groves on the coast of day,
Chasing each other sportively.

III

There would be neither moon nor star;
But the waves would twang like a wet guitar—
Low thunder and thrum in the darkness grum—
  Neither moon nor star;
We would shriek aloud in the dismal dales—
Shriek at each other and squawk and squeal,
  "All night!" rakishly, rakishly;
They would pelt me with oysters and
   wiggletails,
Laughing and clapping their hands at me,
  "All night!" prankishly, prankishly;
But I would toss them back in mine,
Lobsters and turtles of quaint design;
Then leaping out in an abrupt way,
I'd snatch them bald in my devilish glee,
And skip away when they snatched at me,
  Fiendishly, fiendishly.
O, what a jolly life I'd lead,
Ah, what a "bang-up" life indeed!
Soft are the mermaids under the sea—
We would live merrily, merrily.

THE RAINY MORNING

THE dawn of the day was dreary,
    And the lowering clouds o'erhead
Wept in a silent sorrow
    Where the sweet sunshine lay dead;
And a wind came out of the eastward
    Like an endless sigh of pain,
And the leaves fell down in the pathway
    And writhed in the falling rain.

I had tried in a brave endeavor
    To chord my harp with the sun,
But the strings would slacken ever,
    And the task was a weary one:
And so, like a child impatient
    And sick of a discontent,
I bowed in a shower of tear-drops
    And mourned with the instrument.

And lo! as I bowed, the splendor
    Of the sun bent over me,
With a touch as warm and tender
    As a father's hand might be:
And, even as I felt its presence,
    My clouded soul grew bright,
And the tears, like the rain of morning,
    Melted in mists of light.

WE ARE NOT ALWAYS GLAD WHEN
WE SMILE

WE are not always glad when we smile:
　　Though we wear a fair face and are gay,
　And the world we deceive
　May not ever believe
We could laugh in a happier way.—
Yet, down in the deeps of the soul,
　Ofttimes, with our faces aglow,
　　There's an ache and a moan
　　That we know of alone,
　And as only the hopeless may know.

We are not always glad when we smile,—
　For the heart, in a tempest of pain,
　　May live in the guise
　　Of a smile in the eyes
　As a rainbow may live in the rain;
And the stormiest night of our woe
　May hang out a radiant star
　　Whose light in the sky
　　Of despair is a lie
　As black as the thunder-clouds are.

238

We are not always glad when we smile!—
　　But the conscience is quick to record,
　　　All the sorrow and sin
　　　We are hiding within
　　Is plain in the sight of the Lord:
And ever, O ever, till pride
　　And evasion shall cease to defile
　　　The sacred recess
　　　Of the soul, we confess
　　We are not always glad when we smile.

A SUMMER SUNRISE

AFTER LEE O. HARRIS

THE master-hand whose pencils trace
    This wondrous landscape of the morn,
Is but the sun, whose glowing face
Reflects the rapture and the grace
    Of inspiration Heaven-born.

And yet with vision-dazzled eyes,
    I see the lotus-lands of old,
Where odorous breezes fall and rise,
And mountains, peering in the skies,
    Stand ankle-deep in lakes of gold.

And, spangled with the shine and shade,
    I see the rivers raveled out
In strands of silver, slowly fade
In threads of light along the glade
    Where truant roses hide and pout.

240

The tamarind on gleaming sands
  Droops drowsily beneath the heat;
And bowed as though aweary, stands
The stately palm, with lazy hands
  That fold their shadows round his feet.

And mistily, as through a veil,
  I catch the glances of a sea
Of sapphire, dimpled with a gale
Toward Colch's blowing, where the sail
  Of Jason's Argo beckons me.

And gazing on and farther yet,
  I see the isles enchanted, bright
With fretted spire and parapet,
And gilded mosque and minaret,
  That glitter in the crimson light.

But as I gaze, the city's walls
  Are keenly smitten with a gleam
Of pallid splendor, that appalls
The fancy as the ruin falls
  In ashen embers of a dream.

Yet over all the waking earth
  The tears of night are brushed away,
And eyes are lit with love and mirth,
And benisons of richest worth
  Go up to bless the new-born day.

DAS KRIST KINDEL

I HAD fed the fire and stirred it, till the sparkles
    in delight
Snapped their saucy little fingers at the chill De-
    cember night;
And in dressing-gown and slippers, I had tilted back
    "my throne"—
The old split-bottomed rocker—and was musing all
    alone.

I could hear the hungry Winter prowling round the
    outer door,
And the tread of muffled footsteps on the white
    piazza floor;
But the sounds came to me only as the murmur of
    a stream
That mingled with the current of a lazy-flowing
    dream.

Like a fragrant incense rising, curled the smoke of
    my cigar,
With the lamplight gleaming through it like a mist-
    enfolded star;—

And as I gazed, the vapor like a curtain rolled away,
With a sound of bells that tinkled, and the clatter
    of a sleigh.

And in a vision, painted like a picture in the air,
I saw the elfish figure of a man with frosty hair—
A quaint old man that chuckled with a laugh as he
    appeared,
And with ruddy cheeks like embers in the ashes of
    his beard.

He poised himself grotesquely, in an attitude of
    mirth,
On a damask-covered hassock that was sitting on
    the hearth;
And at a magic signal of his stubby little thumb,
I saw the fireplace changing to a bright proscenium.

And looking there, I marveled as I saw a mimic
    stage
Alive with little actors of a very tender age;
And some so very tiny that they tottered as they
    walked,
And lisped and purled and gurgled like the brook-
    lets, when they talked.

And their faces were like lilies, and their eyes like
    purest dew,
And their tresses like the shadows that the shine is
    woven through;

And they each had little burdens, and a little tale
    to tell
Of fairy lore, and giants, and delights delectable.

And they mixed and intermingled, weaving melody
    with joy,
Till the magic circle clustered round a blooming
    baby-boy;
And they threw aside their treasures in an ecstacy
    of glee,
And bent, with dazzled faces and with parted lips,
    to see.

'Twas a wondrous little fellow, with a dainty dou-
    ble-chin,
And chubby cheeks, and dimples for the smiles to
    blossom in;
And he looked as ripe and rosy, on his bed of straw
    and reeds,
As a mellow little pippin that had tumbled in the
    weeds.

And I saw the happy mother, and a group sur-
    rounding her
That knelt with costly presents of frankincense and
    myrrh;
And I thrilled with awe and wonder, as a murmur
    on the air
Came drifting o'er the hearing in a melody of
    prayer:—

By the splendor in the heavens, and the hush upon
    the sea,
And the majesty of silence reigning over Galilee,—
We feel Thy kingly presence, and we humbly bow
    the knee
And lift our hearts and voices in gratefulness to
    Thee.

Thy messenger has spoken, and our doubts have
    fled and gone
As the dark and spectral shadows of the night be-
    fore the dawn;
And, in the kindly shelter of the light around us
    drawn,
We would nestle down forever in the breast we
    lean upon.

You have given us a shepherd—You have given
    us a guide,
And the light of Heaven grew dimmer when You
    sent him from Your side,—
But he comes to lead Thy children where the gates
    will open wide
To welcome his returning when his works are
    glorified.

By the splendor in the heavens, and the hush upon
    the sea,
And the majesty of silence reigning over Galilee,—

*We feel Thy kingly presence, and we humbly bow
    the knee
And lift our hearts and voices in gratefulness to
    Thee.*

Then the vision, slowly failing, with the words of
    the refrain,
Fell swooning in the moonlight through the frosty
    window-pane;
And I heard the clock proclaiming, like an eager
    sentinel
Who brings the world good tidings,—"It is Christ-
    mas—all is well!"

AN OLD YEAR'S ADDRESS

"I HAVE twankled the strings of the twinkering
       rain;
   I have burnished the meteor's mail;
      I have bridled the wind
      When he whinnied and whined
   With a bunch of stars tied to his tail;
But my sky-rocket hopes, hanging over the past,
Must fuzzle and fazzle and fizzle at last!"

I had waded far out in a drizzling dream,
   And my fancies had spattered my eyes
      With a vision of dread,
      With a number ten head,
   And a form of diminutive size—
That wavered and wagged in a singular way
As he wound himself up and proceeded to say,—

"I have trimmed all my corns with the blade of the
       moon;
   I have picked every tooth with a star:
      And I thrill to recall
      That I went through it all
   Like a tune through a tickled guitar.

A—17

247

I have ripped up the rainbow and raveled the ends
When the sun and myself were particular friends."

And pausing again, and producing a sponge
  And wiping the tears from his eyes,
    He sank in a chair
    With a technical air
  That he struggled in vain to disguise,—
For a sigh that he breathed, as I over him leant,
Was haunted and hot with a peppermint scent

"Alas!" he continued in quavering tones
  As a pang rippled over his face,
    "The life was too fast
    For the pleasure to last
  In my very unfortunate case;
And I'm going"—he said as he turned to adjust
A fuse in his bosom,—"I'm going to—BUST!"

I shrieked and awoke with the sullen che-boom
  Of a five-pounder filling my ears;
    And a roseate bloom
    Of a light in the room
  I saw through the mist of my tears,—
But my guest of the night never saw the display,
He had fuzzled and fazzled and fizzled away!

A NEW YEAR'S PLAINT

In words like weeds, I'll wrap me o'er,
  Like coarsest clothes against the cold;
  But that large grief which these enfold
Is given in outline and no more.
                        —TENNYSON.

THE bells that lift their yawning throats
    And lolling tongues with wrangling cries
Flung up in harsh, discordant notes,
    As though in anger, at the skies,—
Are filled with echoings replete,
    With purest tinkles of delight—
So I would have a something sweet
    Ring in the song I sing to-night.

As when a blotch of ugly guise
    On some poor artist's naked floor
Becomes a picture in his eyes,
    And he forgets that he is poor,—
So I look out upon the night,
    That ushers in the dawning year,
And in a vacant blur of light
    I see these fantasies appear.

I see a home whose windows gleam
  Like facets of a mighty gem
That some poor king's distorted dream
  Has fastened in his diadem.
And I behold a throng that reels
  In revelry of dance and mirth,
With hearts of love beneath their heels,
  And in their bosoms hearts of earth.

O Luxury, as false and grand
  As in the mystic tales of old,
When genii answered man's command,
  And built of nothing halls of gold!
O Banquet, bright with pallid jets,
  And tropic blooms, and vases caught
In palms of naked statuettes,
  Ye can not color as ye ought!

For, crouching in the storm without,
  I see the figure of a child,
In little ragged roundabout,
  Who stares with eyes that never smiled—
And he, in fancy can but taste
  The dainties of the kingly fare,
And pick the crumbs that go to waste
  Where none have learned to kneel in prayer.

Go, Pride, and throw your goblet down—
  The "merry greeting" best appears
On loving lips that never drown
  Its worth but in the wine of tears;

Go, close your coffers like your hearts,
   And shut your hearts against the poor,
Go, strut through all your pretty parts
   But take the "Welcome" from your door.

LUTHER BENSON

AFTER READING HIS AUTOBIOGRAPHY

POOR victim of that vulture curse
   That hovers o'er the universe,
With ready talons quick to strike
In every human heart alike,
And cruel beak to stab and tear
In virtue's vitals everywhere,—
You need no sympathy of mine
To aid you, for a strength divine
Encircles you, and lifts you clear
Above this earthly atmosphere.

And yet I can but call you poor,
As, looking through the open door
Of your sad life, I only see
A broad landscape of misery,
And catch through mists of pitying tears
The ruins of your younger years,
I see a father's shielding arm
Thrown round you in a wild alarm—
Struck down, and powerless to free
Or aid you in your agony.

LUTHER BENSON 253

I see a happy home grow dark
And desolate—the latest spark
Of hope is passing in eclipse—
The prayer upon a mother's lips
Has fallen with her latest breath
In ashes on the lips of death—
I see a penitent who reels,
And writhes, and clasps his hands, and
    kneels,
And moans for mercy for the sake
Of that fond heart he dared to break.

And lo! as when in Galilee
A voice above the troubled sea
Commanded "Peace; be still!" the flood
That rolled in tempest-waves of blood
Within you, fell in calm so sweet
It ripples round the Saviour's feet;
And all your noble nature thrilled
With brightest hope and faith, and filled
Your thirsty soul with joy and peace
And praise to Him who gave release.

"DREAM"

BECAUSE her eyes were far too deep
And holy for a laugh to leap
Across the brink where sorrow tried
To drown within the amber tide;
Because the looks, whose ripples kissed
The trembling lids through tender mist,
Were dazzled with a radiant gleam—
Because of this I called her "Dream."

Because the roses growing wild
About her features when she smiled
Were ever dewed with tears that fell
With tenderness ineffable;
Because her lips might spill a kiss
That, dripping in a world like this,
Would tincture death's myrrh-bitter stream
To sweetness—so I called her "Dream."

Because I could not understand
The magic touches of a hand
That seemed, beneath her strange control,
To smooth the plumage of the soul

And calm it, till, with folded wings,
It half forgot its flutterings,
And, nestled in her palm, did seem
To trill a song that called her "Dream."

Because I saw her, in a sleep
As dark and desolate and deep
And fleeting as the taunting night
That flings a vision of delight
To some lorn martyr as he lies
In slumber ere the day he dies—
Because she vanished like a gleam
Of glory, do I call her "Dream."

WHEN EVENING SHADOWS FALL

WHEN evening shadows fall,
   She hangs her cares away
Like empty garments on the wall
   That hides her from the day;
And while old memories throng,
   And vanished voices call,
She lifts her grateful heart in song
   When evening shadows fall.

Her weary hands forget
   The burdens of the day.
The weight of sorrow and regret
   In music rolls away;
And from the day's dull tomb,
   That holds her in its thrall,
Her soul springs up in lily bloom
   When evening shadows fall.

O weary heart and hand,
   Go bravely to the strife—
No victory is half so grand
   As that which conquers life!

One day shall yet be thine—
  The day that waits for all
Whose prayerful eyes are things divine
  When evening shadows fall.

YLLADMAR

HER hair was, oh, so dense a blur
　　Of darkness, midnight envied her;
And stars grew dimmer in the skies
To see the glory of her eyes;
And all the summer rain of light
That showered from the moon at night
Fell o'er her features as the gloom
Of twilight o'er a lily-bloom.

The crimson fruitage of her lips
Was ripe and lush with sweeter wine
Than burgundy or muscadine
Or vintage that the burgher sips
In some old garden on the Rhine:
And I to taste of it could well
Believe my heart a crucible
Of molten love—and I could feel
The drunken soul within me reel
And rock and stagger till it fell.

258

And do you wonder that I bowed
Before her splendor as a cloud
Of storm the golden-sandaled sun
Had set his conquering foot upon?
And did she will it, I could lie
In writhing rapture down and die
A death so full of precious pain
I'd waken up to die again.

A FANTASY

A FANTASY that came to me
    As wild and wantonly designed
As ever any dream might be
    Unraveled from a madman's mind,—
A tangle-work of tissue, wrought
    By cunning of the spider-brain,
    And woven, in an hour of pain,
To trap the giddy flies of thought.

I stood beneath a summer moon
    All swollen to uncanny girth,
And hanging, like the sun at noon,
    Above the center of the earth;
    But with a sad and sallow light,
    As it had sickened of the night
And fallen in a pallid swoon.
Around me I could hear the rush
    Of sullen winds, and feel the whir
Of unseen wings apast me brush
    Like phantoms round a sepulcher;
And, like a carpeting of plush,

A lawn unrolled beneath my feet,
Bespangled o'er with flowers as sweet
To look upon as those that nod
Within the garden-fields of God,
But odorless as those that blow
In ashes in the shades below.

And on my hearing fell a storm
  Of gusty music, sadder yet
  Than every whimper of regret
That sobbing utterance could form,
  And patched with scraps of sound that seemed
  Torn out of tunes that demons dreamed,
  And pitched to such a piercing key,
  It stabbed the ear with agony;
  And when at last it lulled and died,
  I stood aghast and terrified.
I shuddered and I shut my eyes,
  And still could see, and feel aware
  Some mystic presence waited there;
And staring, with a dazed surprise,
  I saw a creature so divine
  That never subtle thought of mine
  May reproduce to inner sight
  So fair a vision of delight.

A syllable of dew that drips
From out a lily's laughing lips
Could not be sweeter than the word
I listened to, yet never heard.—

For, oh, the woman hiding there
Within the shadows of her hair,
Spake to me in an undertone
So delicate, my soul alone
But understood it as a moan
Of some weak melody of wind
A heavenward breeze had left behind.

A tracery of trees, grotesque
   Against the sky, behind her seen,
Like shapeless shapes of arabesque
   Wrought in an Oriental screen;
And tall, austere and statuesque
    She loomed before it—e'en as though
    The spirit-hand of Angelo
    Had chiseled her to life complete,
    With chips' of moonshine round her feet.
And I grew jealous of the dusk,
   To see it softly touch her face,
   As lover-like, with fond embrace,
It folded round her like a husk:
But when the glitter of her hand,
   Like wasted glory, beckoned me,
   My eyes grew blurred and dull and dim—
   My vision failed—I could not see—
I could not stir—I could but stand,
   Till, quivering in every limb,
   I flung me prone, as though to swim

The tide of grass whose waves of green
Went rolling ocean-wide between
My helpless shipwrecked heart and her
Who claimed me for a worshiper.

And writhing thus in my despair,
  I heard a weird, unearthly sound,
  That seemed to lift me from the ground
And hold me floating in the air.
I looked, and lo! I saw her bow
  Above a harp within her hands;
A crown of blossoms bound her brow,
  And on her harp were twisted strands
Of silken starlight, rippling o'er
With music never heard before
By mortal ears; and, at the strain,
I felt my Spirit snap its chain
And break away,—and I could see
It as it turned and fled from me
To greet its mistress, where she smiled
To see the phantom dancing wild
And wizard-like before the spell
Her mystic fingers knew so well.

A DREAM

I DREAMED I was a spider;
  A big, fat, hungry spider;
A lusty, rusty spider
  With a dozen palsied limbs;
With a dozen limbs that dangled
Where three wretched flies were tangled
And their buzzing wings were strangled
  In the middle of their hymns.

And I mocked them like a demon—
A demoniacal demon
Who delights to be a demon
  For the sake of sin alone;
And with fondly false embraces
Did I weave my mystic laces
Round their horror-stricken faces
  Till I muffled every groan.

And I smiled to see them weeping,
For to see an insect weeping,
Sadly, sorrowfully weeping,
  Fattens every spider's mirth;

And to note a fly's heart quaking,
And with anguish ever aching
Till you see it slowly breaking
  Is the sweetest thing on earth.

I experienced a pleasure,
Such a highly-flavored pleasure,
Such intoxicating pleasure,
  That I drank of it like wine;
And my mortal soul engages
That no spider on the pages
Of the history of ages
  Felt a rapture more divine.

I careened around and capered—
Madly, mystically capered—
For three days and nights I capered
  Round my web in wild delight;
Till with fierce ambition burning,
And an inward thirst and yearning
I hastened my returning
  With a fiendish appetite.

And I found my victims dying,
"Ha!" they whispered, "we are dying!"
Faintly whispered, "we are dying,
  And our earthly course is run."
And the scene was so impressing
That I breathed a special blessing,
As I killed them with caressing
  And devoured them one by one.

DREAMER, SAY

DREAMER, say, will you dream for me
    A wild sweet dream of a foreign land,
Whose border sips of a foaming sea
    With lips of coral and silver sand;
Where warm winds loll on the shady deeps,
    Or lave themselves in the tearful mist
The great wild wave of the breaker weeps
    O'er crags of opal and amethyst?

Dreamer, say, will you dream a dream
    Of tropic shades in the lands of shine,
Where the lily leans o'er an amber stream
    That flows like a rill of wasted wine,—
Where the palm-trees, lifting their shields of
       green,
    Parry the shafts of the Indian sun
Whose splintering vengeance falls between
    The reeds below where the waters run?

Dreamer, say, will you dream of love
  That lives in a land of sweet perfume,
Where the stars drip down from the skies above
  In molten spatters of bud and bloom?
Where never the weary eyes are wet,
  And never a sob in the balmy air,
And only the laugh of the paroquet
  Breaks the sleep of the silence there?

BRYANT

THE harp has fallen from the master's hand;
   Mute is the music, voiceless are the strings,
   Save such faint discord as the wild wind flings
In sad Æolian murmurs through the land.
The tide of melody, whose billows grand
   Flowed o'er the world in clearest utterings,
   Now, in receding current, sobs and sings
That song we never wholly understand.
* * O, eyes where glorious prophecies belong,
   And gracious reverence to humbly bow,
And kingly spirit, proud, and pure, and strong;
   O, pallid minstrel with the laureled brow,
And lips so long attuned to sacred song,
   How sweet must be the Heavenly anthem now!

BABYHOOD

HEIGH-HO! Babyhood! Tell me where you
    linger!
Let's toddle home again, for we have gone astray;
Take this eager hand of mine and lead me by the
    finger
Back to the lotus-lands of the far-away!

Turn back the leaves of life.—Don't read the
    story.—
Let's find the pictures, and fancy all the rest;
We can fill the written pages with a brighter glory
Than old Time, the story-teller, at his very best.

Turn to the brook where the honeysuckle tipping
    O'er its vase of perfume spills it on the breeze,
And the bee and humming-bird in ecstacy are sip-
    ping
    From the fairy flagons of the blooming locust-
    trees.

Turn to the lane where we used to "teeter-totter,"
  Printing little foot-palms in the mellow mold—
Laughing at the lazy cattle wading in the water
  Where the ripples dimple round the buttercups of
    gold;

Where the dusky turtle lies basking on the gravel
  Of the sunny sand-bar in the middle tide,
And the ghostly dragon-fly pauses in his travel
  To rest like a blossom where the water-lily died.

Heigh-ho! Babyhood! Tell me where you linger!
  Let's toddle home again, for we have gone astray;
Take this eager hand of mine and lead me by the
    finger
  Back to the lotus-lands of the far-away!

LIBERTY

NEW CASTLE, JULY 4, 1878

I

FOR a hundred years the pulse of time
  Has throbbed for Liberty;
For a hundred years the grand old clime
  Columbia has been free;
    For a hundred years our country's love,
    The Stars and Stripes, has waved above.

Away far out on the gulf of years—
  Misty and faint and white
Through the fogs of wrong—a sail appears,
  And the Mayflower heaves in sight,
    And drifts again, with its little flock
    Of a hundred souls, on Plymouth Rock.

Do you see them there—as long, long since—
  Through the lens of History;

A—19   271

Do you see them there as their chieftain prints
  In the snow his bended knee,
    And lifts his voice through the wintry blast
    In thanks for a peaceful home at last?

Though the skies are dark and the coast is bleak,
  And the storm is wild and fierce,
Its frozen flake on the upturned cheek
  Of the Pilgrim melts in tears,
    And the dawn that springs from the darkness
      there
    Is the morning light of an answered prayer.

The morning light of the day of Peace
  That gladdens the aching eyes,
And gives to the soul that sweet release
  That the present verifies,—
    Nor a snow so deep, nor a wind so chill
    To quench the flame of a freeman's will!

II

Days of toil when the bleeding hand
  Of the pioneer grew numb,
When the untilled tracts of the barren land
  Where the weary ones had come
    Could offer nought from a fruitful soil
    To stay the strength of the stranger's toil.

Days of pain, when the heart beat low,
  And the empty hours went by
Pitiless, with the wail of woe
  And the moan of Hunger's cry—
    When the trembling hands upraised in prayer
    Had only the strength to hold them there.

Days when the voice of hope had fled—
  Days when the eyes grown weak
Were folded to, and the tears they shed
  Were frost on a frozen cheek—
    When the storm bent down from the skies
      and gave
    A shroud of snow for the Pilgrim's grave.

Days at last when the smiling sun
  Glanced down from a summer sky,
And a music rang where the rivers run,
  And the waves went laughing by;
    And the rose peeped over the mossy bank
    While the wild deer stood in the stream and
      drank.

And the birds sang out so loud and good,
  In a symphony so clear
And pure and sweet that the woodman stood
  With his ax upraised to hear,
    And to shape the words of the tongue unknown
    Into a language all his own:—

1

Sing! every bird, to-day!
  Sing for the sky so clear,
  And the gracious breath of the atmosphere
Shall waft our cares away.
Sing! sing! for the sunshine free;
Sing through the land from sea to sea;
Lift each voice in the highest key
  And sing for Liberty!

2

Sing for the arms that fling
  Their fetters in the dust
  And lift their hands in higher trust
Unto the one Great King;
Sing for the patriot heart and hand;
Sing for the country they have planned;
Sing that the world may understand
  This is Freedom's land!

3

Sing in the tones of prayer,
  Sing till the soaring soul
  Shall float above the world's control
In Freedom everywhere!

Sing for the good that is to be,
Sing for the eyes that are to see
The land where man at last is free,
   O sing for Liberty!

III

A holy quiet reigned, save where the hand
Of labor sent a murmur through the land,
And happy voices in a harmony
Taught every lisping breeze a melody.
A nest of cabins, where the smoke upcurled
A breathing incense to the other world.
A land of languor from the sun of noon,
That fainted slowly to the pallid moon,
Till stars, thick-scattered in the garden-land
Of Heaven by the great Jehovah's hand,
Had blossomed into light to look upon
The dusky warrior with his arrow drawn,
As skulking from the covert of the night
With serpent cunning and a fiend's delight,
With murderous spirit, and a yell of hate
The voice of Hell might tremble to translate:
When the fond mother's tender lullaby
Went quavering in shrieks all suddenly,
And baby-lips were dabbled with the stain
Of crimson at the bosom of the slain,
And peaceful homes and fortunes ruined—lost
In smoldering embers of the holocaust.

Yet on and on, through years of gloom and strife,
Our country struggled into stronger life;
Till colonies, like footprints in the sand,
Marked Freedom's pathway winding through the
      land—
And not the footprints to be swept away
Before the storm we hatched in Boston Bay,—
But footprints where the path of war begun
That led to Bunker Hill and Lexington,—
For he who "dared to lead where others dared
To follow" found the promise there declared
Of Liberty, in blood of Freedom's host
Baptized to Father, Son, and Holy Ghost!

Oh, there were times when every patriot breast
Was riotous with sentiments expressed
In tones that swelled in volume till the sound
Of lusty war itself was well-nigh drowned.
Oh, those were times when happy eyes with tears
Brimmed o'er as all the misty doubts and fears
Were washed away, and Hope with gracious mien,
Reigned from her throne again a sovereign queen,
Until at last, upon a day like this
When flowers were blushing at the summer's kiss,
And when the sky was cloudless as the face
Of some sweet infant in its angel grace,—
There came a sound of music, thrown afloat
Upon the balmy air—a clanging note
Reiterated from the brazen throat

Of Independence Bell: A sound so sweet,
The clamoring throngs of people in the streets
Were stilled as at the solemn voice of prayer,
And heads were bowed, and lips were moving there
That made no sound—until the spell had passed,
And then, as when all sudden comes the blast
Of some tornado, came the cheer on cheer
Of every eager voice, while far and near
The echoing bells upon the atmosphere
Set glorious rumors floating, till the ear
Of every listening patriot tingled clear,
And thrilled with joy and jubilee to hear.

1

Stir all your echoes up,
  O Independence Bell,
And pour from your inverted cup
  The song we love so well.

Lift high your happy voice,
  And swing your iron tongue
Till syllables of praise rejoice
  That never yet were sung.

Ring in the gleaming dawn
  Of Freedom—Toll the knell
Of Tyranny, and then ring on,
  O Independence Bell.—

Ring on, and drown the moan
Above the patriot slain,
Till sorrow's voice shall catch the tone
And join the glad refrain.

Ring out the wounds of wrong
And rankle in the breast;
Your music like a slumber-song
Will lull revenge to rest.

Ring out from Occident
To Orient, and peal
From continent to continent
The mighty joy you feel.

Ring! Independence Bell!
Ring on till worlds to be
Shall listen to the tale you tell
Of love and Liberty!

IV

O Liberty—the dearest word
A bleeding country ever heard,—
We lay our hopes upon thy shrine
And offer up our lives for thine.
You gave us many happy years
Of peace and plenty ere the tears
A mourning country wept were dried
Above the graves of those who died

Upon thy threshold. And again
When newer wars were bred, and men
Went marching in the cannon's breath
And died for thee and loved the death,
While, high above them, gleaming bright,
The dear old flag remained in sight,
And lighted up their dying eyes
With smiles that brightened paradise.
O Liberty, it is thy power
To gladden us in every hour
Of gloom, and lead us by thy hand
As little children through a land
Of bud and blossom; while the days
Are filled with sunshine, and thy praise
Is warbled in the roundelays
Of joyous birds, and in the song
Of waters, murmuring along
The paths of peace, whose flowery fringe
Has roses finding deeper tinge
Of crimson, looking on themselves
Reflected—leaning from the shelves
Of cliff and crag and mossy mound
Of emerald splendor shadow-drowned.—
We hail thy presence, as you come
With bugle blast and rolling drum,
And booming guns and shouts of glee
Commingled in a symphony
That thrills the worlds that throng to see
The glory of thy pageantry.

And with thy praise, we breathe a prayer
That God who leaves you in our care
May favor us from this day on
With thy dear presence—till the dawn
Of Heaven, breaking on thy face,
Lights up thy first abiding place.

TOM VAN ARDEN

TOM VAN ARDEN, my old friend,
  Our warm fellowship is one
Far too old to comprehend
  Where its bond was first begun:
    Mirage-like before my gaze
    Gleams a land of other days,
    Where two truant boys, astray,
    Dream their lazy lives away.

There's a vision, in the guise
  Of Midsummer, where the Past
Like a weary beggar lies
  In the shadow Time has cast;
    And as blends the bloom of trees
    With the drowsy hum of bees,
    Fragrant thoughts and murmurs blend,
    Tom Van Arden, my old friend.

Tom Van Arden, my old friend,
  All the pleasures we have known
Thrill me now as I extend
  This old hand and grasp your own—

Feeling, in the rude caress,
All affection's tenderness;
Feeling, though the touch be rough,
Our old souls are soft enough.

So we'll make a mellow hour:
　Fill your pipe, and taste the wine—
Warp your face, if it be sour,
　I can spare a smile from mine;
　　If it sharpen up your wit,
　　Let me feel the edge of it—
　　I have eager ears to lend,
　　Tom Van Arden, my old friend.

Tom Van Arden, my old friend,
　Are we "lucky dogs," indeed?
Are we all that we pretend
　In the jolly life we lead?—
　　Bachelors, we must confess,
　　Boast of "single blessedness"
　　To the world, but not alone—
　　Man's best sorrow is his own!

And the saddest truth is this,—
　Life to us has never proved
What we tasted in the kiss
　Of the women we have loved:
　　Vainly we congratulate
　　Our escape from such a fate
　　As their lying lips could send,
　　Tom Van Arden, my old friend!

Tom Van Arden, my old friend,
  Hearts, like fruit upon the stem,
Ripen sweetest, I contend,
  As the frost falls over them:
    Your regard for me to-day
    Makes November taste of May,
    And through every vein of rhyme
    Pours the blood of summer-time.

When our souls are cramped with youth
  Happiness seems far away
In the future, while, in truth,
  We look back on it to-day
    Through our tears, nor dare to boast,—
    "Better to have loved and lost!"
    Broken hearts are hard to mend,
    Tom Van Arden, my old friend.

Tom Van Arden, my old friend,
  I grow prosy, and you tire;
Fill the glasses while I bend
  To prod up the failing fire. . . .
    You are restless:—I presume
    There's a dampness in the room.—
    Much of warmth our nature begs,
    With rheumatics in our legs! . . .

Humph! the legs we used to fling
  Limber-jointed in the dance,
When we heard the fiddle ring
  Up the curtain of Romance,

And in crowded public halls
Played with hearts like juggler's balls.—
Feats of mountebanks, depend!—
Tom Van Arden, my old friend.

Tom Van Arden, my old friend,
  Pardon, then, this theme of mine:
While the firelight leaps to lend
  Higher color to the wine,—
    I propose a health to those
    Who have *homes,* and home's repose,
    Wife- and child-love without end!
      . . . Tom Van Arden, my old friend.